Village Kid

And Other Ramblings

June McCleave

HERMITAGE
publishing

First published by Hermitage Publishing 2023

ISBN: 978-1-80352-829-8

Book formatted by Antony Wootten

Front cover photograph:

Blue Hall, The Holme, Great Broughton

For my dear childhood, and lifelong, friends,

Carole and Joan,

who were there for me and understood.

Contents

"Life's Experiences Can Be Transformed, Or Transformative"

Ronnie Kirk, local preacher, Stokesley Methodist Church

Billy Collins, writer, poet and Master Class tutor said, "Everyone has a story to tell. Write about what you know." So that is what I have done, following his good advice.

In my heart, I have always known I had a story to tell, the problem being, getting started and finding the time to do it. Also, I now feel that I can share the reality without experiencing the pain and shame I would have felt when I was younger. I now know that none of it was my fault.

Retirement has afforded me the ability to surmount these obstacles.

So here goes.

My book is in two sections, the first being autobiographical, based on a childhood full of fun, adventure and pain, and the second, Other Ramblings, is an anthology of poetry which I have written over the years, in addition to other pieces of creative writing which I felt I wanted to include.

He asked me to marry him. I was 18 and he was 85. He told me that it was better to be "an old man's sweetheart than a young man's slave" He offered me all his worldly goods: house, car, money, possessions. Needless to say I declined, but as sensitively as I could. My pragmatic mother advised that it was "only an old man's fancy" She wasn't shocked. I thought that she might have been. When I married, at 23, in 1973, he wouldn't come to my wedding.

As I was growing up I had visited him, and his invalid wife, shopping for them, washing windows and even painting upstairs window frames, at the top of a ladder, for a bit of spending money. It all mounted up. There was no pocket money in our house, in fact, no spare money at all. You had to get out and earn it. That maxim has remained with me all of my life, You don't get "owt for nowt" At the end, when she was dying, I sat beside her bed and helped to feed her. He lacked the patience.

Years earlier, he had tried to trap me in the corner of the dining room, one Xmas celebration, when all the family, and guests, were ensconced in another room well away from my sojourn into the kitchen. I challenged him loudly, "What do you think you are doing?" He let me go. Noone ever knew. I was very young, but instinctively knew something was very wrong and he shouldn't be trying to get hold of me.

My sister had had a similar experience when she was sent to pick up a pint of milk from the local milkman. It was a hot day and she was wearing a very unflattering swimsuit. She was cornered by the said milkman in his milking parlour but had the presence of mind to quickly duck under his arm and escape. Needless to say she was never sent there again. She would be 7 or 8 when this happened. If we ran out of milk my mother went to collect it. I doubt he would have had the nerve to try it on with her!!

My shopping round took me in to many houses around Great Broughton: Walter and Ana Baimbridge, Lizzie Baimbridge, Annie and Jack Skilbeck (my aunt and uncle) Eric Clarkson, Granny and Grandad Cousans and Lilian Featherstone, to name but a few. They paid me to go to Brough's shop for them, 2 pennies a trip. The 2 pennies mounted up and paid for Xmas and birthday presents from The Little Shop in the village (run by the Reeves family) where you could save, all year, in their Xmas Club. At the age of 7/8 I had established a sizeable "round" and was quite the entrepreneur.

On a particular occasion, I was shopping for a lady my mother cleaned for. I think she was called Mrs. Coverdale and she lived at Glenside in the High Street. My imagination went quite wild, on that day, and I ordered a heap of groceries nobody had asked for. They were duly delivered to the lady in question, much to her surprise and consternation. Where had it all come from and who had ordered it? Of course, it was me, the culprit. Needless to say, it all had to be sent back with a profuse apology. I doubt that I would be trusted again to go shopping!!

Carol singing was a very necessary, and lucrative, money spinner and my sister, and I, were good at it, both having reasonably melodic voices. It was exciting going round people's houses, in the dark, with a torch, trying not to fall over obstacles, in the garden and at the front door, or avoiding marauding dogs. We sang to our heart's content and were well received.

Miss Turton, who lived at the top of the village, would only have Margaret, and I, to sing carols for her. We would warble in her sitting room and she would give us 2 shillings and sixpence each, an absolute fortune I can tell you. Yes, Miss Turton was well worth a visit!

Further up the village, towards The Cleveland Hills, was Sanderson's farm and, at Xmas time, the big barn was filled with turkeys, chickens (dead) and pluckers. Feathers filled the air and were attached to clothing and hair, generally getting everywhere. We stood in the big barn and sang loudly, usually provoking a good round of applause and more dosh. Home we would go and share it all out . Great fun. Freedom afforded to us that wouldn't be to today's kids.

Lucky Birding was another village tradition, executed on New Year's morning. The Lucky Birder was supposed to be a dark haired boy who carried a piece of coal and was first over the threshold. Well, we girls, wanted a look in and the chance to fill our pockets with Xmas cake, sweets and fruit. So we would start early on our tour of the village families, beating the boys to it, and shouting loudly,

Lucky bird, Lucky bird
Chuck, chuck, chuck
Master and Missus
It's time to get up.
If you don't get up
You'll have no luck
So please will you give me
My New Year's gift.

The bleary-eyed occupants weren't too concerned with the niceties of us being the wrong sex, they just wanted rid of us so paid up. Others were very generous, invited us in, and as well as plying us with sweets, nuts, Xmas cake and mince pies, we were also offered a glass of homemade ginger beer. Needless to say, we didn't stand on the scales after the gorging. After it all our pockets were coated with all sorts of unspeakable gunge. Happy times and happy memories.

Miss Elcoate has to be mentioned in my reminiscences. She was a true village character who lived in The Holme with Dicky Shaw (uncertain regarding the relationship between the two!!) She possessed a few yellow teeth and had tightly drawn back hair, in a bun. Lots of white whiskers protruded from her chin and upper lip which fascinated me. She had quite a witchy cackle when something amused her. If the truth be known, she frightened me to death, but I also found her quaint and mesmerising. Whenever you visited her house, probably to buy her free range eggs, the smell of the homemade bread, rising before the fire in great earthenware bowls , would greet your nostrils. When bread wasn't rising, on the hearth, cardboard boxes filled with new born piglets, could be found, probably this being the warmest place in the house (no central heating then!)

Miss Elcoate lived on a farm, with extensive fields, behind her house which bordered on to my Grandparents' land at Blue Hall. Much work had been invested in the harvest and the haystacks stood proudly, ready to be gathered in. One day, we naughty kids decided to leapfrog over the stacks, knocking some down and doing damage. Fun for us, but very dangerous, if we got caught. The next visit for eggs I was challenged. Was I one of the culprits?

"Oh no Miss Elcoate, it wasn't me. I wasn't among the gang who did it." What a little fibber. Sorry Miss Elcoate if you're up there listening.

As you will have gathered, money was a vitally important component for a young girl growing up and requiring certain feminine necessities. Every penny had to be earned and this resulted in me juggling a number of tasks, some of which had to be pruned back when I was studying for GCE's and A levels.

The numerous babysitting jobs I had, looking after affluent families' kids (Spark's, Gloag's, Jones', Moira's, Sockett's etc.) brought in 10 shillings a night and that involved an overnight sleep. This was a thoroughly good deal, from my point of view, because I had a lovely, comfy bed, a hot bath in a bathroom (remember we had a tin bath in front of the fire, at home) and a scrumptious supper and breakfast the next morning. On a Saturday morning I cleaned and ironed for Mrs. Jones earning another 10 shillings.

At one point I was collecting eggs, in a very smelly barn, at Burgess's farm, which was situated at the foot of The Wainstones. My dear friend, Joan Carveth, helped me. Conditions weren't good, some birds were dying, so this job was short lived as my mother felt it was a bit of a health hazard.

The Countryside Restaurant, now known as The Wainstones Hotel, provided me with my main income as a waitress. 2 shillings and sixpence an hour, shared tips with the management. The working hours were quite challenging, starting the day at 8.00 with breakfasts, merging into morning coffees and on to lunches. A break in the early afternoon was followed by serving afternoon teas and then on to dinner. Sometimes I would be working late into the evening or even early morning. Exhausting. Something had to give if I was going to be prepared for exams and remain sane. So, the hours were reduced and eventually I left when I went to college.

Wheldon's farm, at the watersplash end of The Holme, was our playground and adventure focus. Poor Mrs. Wheldon already had an enormous family of her own and must have been truly fed up when my sister, and I, were such regular visitors. We loved it there: driving the tractor, totally illegal, building dens in old, flea ridden hen houses, helping to bring the cows in for milking by shouting, " Cush up," playing Hide and Seek in the hay shed and my sister devised a game called Kickory which, in effect, was Hide and Seek, in the dark, using a torch, around the farm yard. Highly dangerous but enormous fun. How one of us didn't get seriously injured, I'll never know.

Mrs. Wheldon always appeared careworn and exhausted with never ending washing, baking, cooking, bed making, cleaning and chamber pot emptying. Poor woman. She certainly could have done without us, in her house, playing endless games of Monopoly and playing music loudly. I was enthralled to see that their earth toilet had four holes of varying sizes, whereas ours only had two, enabling the whole family to sit there together. I can hear her saying now,

"Haven't you kids got homes of your own to go to?" Of course, we did, but it was much more fun on the Wheldon farm.

In front of the farm was a steep, winding, uneven road leading down to the water splash. Our gang was very proficient at constructing "Bogeys" out of discarded pram wheels and planks of wood, skilfully nailed together. Two, or three of us, would ensconce ourselves on the Bogey, hanging on for dear life, then we would push off at the top of the hill, gathering speed as we negotiated the bends and bumps. At the bottom we hit the water with an almighty splash and would end up thoroughly drenched from the spray or the whole contraption would skid through the water, tipping us all off for a total soaking. Home we would go for dry clothes and a scolding. But it didn't deter us in the least. Next day we would be back at it again.

The Warren - Our Magic Place

If you walk from Kirby in Cleveland to the foot of the Cleveland Hills, you will encounter a gate, at the end of the road, and, inside that gate is "The Warren," our truly magical place and our sheep- scattered playground, as we grew up.

There wasn't much room in our two up two down Jet Miners cottage for play, but, my goodness, that was amply compensated for by the surrounding countryside which created a truly amazing environment for fresh air, exercise, and, most of all, the foundation for our imaginations to run wild and flourish.

We spent many happy hours in The Warren, having picnics, rolling paste eggs, which we had lovingly painted, at Easter, playing Hide and Seek in the bracken, building dens, picking wild mushrooms, never entirely sure if they were the edible ones and also collecting sheep droppings.

I feel that I must elaborate on the sheep droppings saga. My father, being an ex-Durham miner, where they took the growing and showing of leeks very seriously, grew enormous leeks to "show" and, in order to grow the winning specimens, the leeks had to be fed with a most obnoxious brew which consisted of sheep droppings, various other secret and unspeakable ingredients and water. The whole hideous concoction was somehow heated in an ancient oil drum, until the consistency was just right. Then it would be fed, directly, into the roots of the leeks. Well, you may not like the sound of it, but I can tell you, those leeks were second to none, particularly the flavour!!!!

One picnic, that we had, as an extended family, with my Aunty Elsie, Uncle Reg, Michael and David James, didn't go quite according to plan as the heavens decided to open just as we were going to tuck into our egg sandwiches. Someone saved the day by erecting a barrier against the downpour using bracken and a tarpaulin. Don't ask me how we came to have a tarpaulin with us, but I guess Uncle Reg had checked the weather forecast and decided to be on the safe side. What fun crouched together, listening to the patter of the rainfall above our heads, chatting and laughing as we filled our faces.

At one point in my family's history, we nearly ended up living in Warren House, which is situated on the top of Warren hill. No running water, no central heating, no flush toilet or bathroom. You can imagine how harsh the conditions would be in the middle of Winter when you would likely be snowed in and the ice would form on the inside of the windows and icicles would be suspended from every available ledge. My astute, and wise, mother declined the offer to rent it because it would have meant a very isolated, and lengthy trek to get to the village school in Great Broughton (or Kirby for my brother) not to mention how you would cope if you ran out of provisions. No quick nip to the shop if you lived up there!!

One of my mother's childhood memories, which she never forgot, and, related, with a warning, to her daughters, was of a young girl being attacked on the road leading up from White Post Corner to the foot of The Wainstones. She wasn't going to risk this happening with her own family.

I do, however, remember a Miss Garbutt living there, on her own. She frightened me one day when I saw her, shrouded in a hooded black cloak, rooting about in the ditch which is now a caravan park. Goodness knows what she was looking for, but I certainly was not hanging about to discover more.

Behind Warren House, and right on the top of the hill, is a very steep slope where we would roll our lovingly painted paste eggs, at Easter. You can imagine what was left by the time they arrived at the bottom, absolutely nothing!! Evidence of the bumpy ride could be seen all the way down the slope with fragments of shell, bits of egg white and yolk easily detected. Certainly, there was nothing left to eat, but it was great fun.

Right at the top of the said hill, was a solitary tree, that I always remember being there, until, one fateful night, when it was struck by lightning during a violent thunderstorm. I was fascinated, and intrigued, to observe the black gash all the way down the length of the trunk. Poor little tree never recovered and, I think, it was completely chopped down in the end, having stood sentinel, for goodness knows how long, as it overlooked the panorama stretching towards Teesside, on a clear day.

Our "gang" had a brilliant game of Hide and Seek amongst the bracken. No concern for slithering snakes (particularly adders) or dangerous spores from the bracken. The idea was that the person hiding found a spot amongst the thickest fronds, and don't forget, this was quite a vast area to choose from. Then the seekers would shout "Shake," and the hider was expected to vigorously shake the bracken where they were concealed. Now, this was all well and good on a calm day, but, on a windy day, it was a real dilemma trying to decide whether it was just a "Shake" or the wind. Eventually, and often after considerable time, the hider would be found (that is if the seekers didn't get bored and clear off home)

I look back on those times, growing up, and playing in The Warren, with such fond memories. Weren't we just so lucky to have it all on our doorstep, our pastoral playground where we had that freedom to disappear all day, with our fellow village children, our mates, our pals. Safety in numbers. To feel the wind in your hair and on your face, pure moorland air. To really know the meaning of friendship. To hear the plaintive cries of lambs and sheep and to also hear the gentle trickling of the moorland springs running down the incline. And, of course, to see the disappearing white bob tails of the numerous rabbits as they bolted for their burrows. After all this magic place is called The Warren.

Memories. Happy, Happy Memories.

Broughton Beck

Sinuating slowly and steadily through this pastoral scene.
A small, and modest village, then.
Swathes of endless playground for the local kids.
Fishing for tiddlers, bullheads and tadpoles
With rustic rods, child created.
Imprisoned then in jam jar jails.

Seasonal transformations.
Skating, in winter, ice capped and cracked.
Icicles suspended from trees and branches.
Tapestries of filigreed snow embroideries, in sparkling whites and blues.
Jack Frost, at work with his nocturnal paintbrush.

Along The Holme, beside our ancestral home,
Blue Hall, the beck beckons to signs of Spring, dabbling
ducks and their fluffy, daffodil- yellow offspring.

On occasion pollution penetrated the clear flow
From farms upstream.

Farmers who did not care.
Not their problem.

Child memory of the day when the herd of cows chased my gang into the woodland.
The tree branch, stretching across the beck
Saved our skins.
We shinnied up and watched, legs dangling.
The bovine bunch prowling frustratedly below.

Village Church of England School, 1955

5 Years Old

IT moulded the clay of my youth.
NOT always kindly or caringly.
SHE was given free reign over our vulnerability.
Sometimes cruel.
Sometimes vindictive.
Sometimes humiliating.
Often isolating.
Always frightening.
SMACKED for whispering.
SMACKED for talking.
SMACKED for forgetting those tables.
SMACKED for not conforming.
SMACKED for the sake of it.
Just smacked.

I was paraded on the teacher's table
for forgetting 12 pence = one shilling, 13 pence = one and a penny etc. etc. etc.

Made to say it   but couldn't.
Couldn't remember it.

A sea of my classmates' faces
Watching
Watching
And feeling my anguish
Glad it wasn't them.
Sent to Coventry for forgetting a hanky.

STAND TO ATTENTION!   THE DAILY INSPECTION.
Teeth   Hair   Shoes   Nails   Hanky
The dreaded hanky I always forgot.

Limited toilet trips.
Hold it in 'till home time.
Hence:
Wet knickers draped around the classroom stove
Steam slowly rising from them.

My sister shadowed her classmate home.
Glaring evidence of dried diarrhoea rivulets
down the back of her legs.

Refused toilet trip by DRACONIAN DRAGON.

It wouldn't happen nowadays

Thank God. Would it ?

Escaping School

I ran away from school quite regularly, but usually was taken back. It was only a short distance, up the road, to reach home.

Probably smacked or chastised, again, by the teacher who was not fit to be in charge of small children. Her teaching methods were adopted to frighten the wits out of her charges. God only knows how we ever learned a thing. But, miraculously, I did, in spite of the constant undermining of confidence, the almost daily smacks, the humiliation of being stood on the teacher's table for forgetting a times table and the sending to Coventry, by the whole school, for forgetting a handkerchief!!

Two teachers were employed at this school, the Headmistress and the one who taught me. Nothing was done to stop her disciplinary methods. She had free rein to do whatever she wished.

She was a large-framed woman and had rather a masculine voice, a hard face and a swinging ponytail. She smelt of chalk and classrooms. She clearly did not like me, but, did have her favourites, usually the daughters of fearsome mothers who she would not be prepared to cross. My mother was obviously not fearsome enough!!!

When I was eleven, I took the eleven plus exam and managed to pass the first half, not enough to earn me a Grammar School place, that came later. I was informed, by the said teacher, that the only reason I had passed, part of the exam, was because of my age and had nothing to do with my ability. Another "downer" administered.

Many of my classmates were also scared of her. Toilet visits were not allowed outside play time and dinner time. Many wet pairs of knickers resulted from this measure, usually hanging around the black fire guard surrounding the classroom stove.

I left at age eleven and discovered that education, and learning, could be fun. I began to "blossom" under the guidance of kinder, more sympathetic, tutors.

Amazingly enough, I spent the next 40 years in the classroom, determined to give my students a more enriching, and positive, experience, than I had, and loved every minute of it.

A Child's Chapel

Great Broughton Methodist Chapel

1952 - 1966

Contents

Introduction

Being born at the foot of the Cleveland Hills, and in the

shadow of the Wainstones, in what at that time was a small village surrounded by green fields, was a real stroke of luck and good fortune.

As children of Great Broughton village, our playground consisted of neighbouring farms, endless stretches of open meadow and softly undulating slopes rising from the village to Hasty Bank, Cold Moor, the Wainstones, and our favourite, the Warren; pathways stretching along to Carlton Bank, jewels indeed to explore with our friends, enjoying family picnics in the sunshine (and sometimes thunderstorms) fishing in the streams, gathering wild flowers and fruit. Marvelling in a freedom of spirit and body that to a certain extent is denied the children of today.

This rustic environment, together with the guidance and teaching at Great Broughton School for Girls, moulded the clay of our youth. The day school teaching worked in close liaison with Sunday School and very often our head mistress, Mrs. Pearson, would attend Chapel and take a mental note of any of her girls who were missing. The following morning at day school you would be expected to give a good account of your absence from Chapel the previous day. Religious education was given just as much emphasis as the 3 Rs. If anything, Chapel had an even greater impact on our development, and from a very young age it supported us with a moral code, an understanding of what was right and wrong and encouraged us to stay on the straight and narrow.

It provided us also with a social life in the form of parties, Christmas celebrations, annual trips to the coast, Whitby or Scarborough, youth club activities, and special occasions like Easter and Chapel Anniversary.

In fact, all in all, it played a vital part in our upbringing and our mother, Bessie Phillips, ensured we attended at least once a day for Sunday School and morning service. She had, herself, been "encouraged" to attend Chapel (the Village Hall) three times every Sunday by her own mother (my grandmother Cecelia Mary Cousans of Blue Hall). Often, I attended evening service with my dear friend Lizzie Bainbridge of Garden House, Great Broughton, (the one with the village pump).

There was always a steady devoted membership of both village children and adults, keeping the life-blood, the heart of the Chapel, beating.

Children on Sunday School Register

- Edwards family: Bernard, Barry, Ron
- Valerie Dodsworth

- Jean and Jennifer and Brian Wheldon
- Jane and Russell Palmer
- Shirley Cooper
- Wendy Smith
- Janet Parkin
- Swales family
- Dilys and Janet Chapman
- Gatenby family: Elaine and Steven
- Pamela and Carol Kitching
- Christine and Marion Leng
- Reed family: Glyn, Gordon and Gavin
- Margaret and June Phillips
- Iain and Alayne Sparks
- Joan Wood

Other regular adult attenders

- The Bainbridges
- The Smiths
- Gwen Smith
- Lizzie Bainbridge
- Cecelia Cousans
- Miss Barthram
- Theresa Whitney

- The Mercers
- Mrs. Garbutt
- Mrs. Lee
- Lilian Featherson
- The MacDonalds
- The Wild family

Preachers

- Reverend Peter Sutcliffe

Names of Lay Preachers

- Bob Swales
- Victor Chapman
- Mr. Dodsworth
- Mr. Bainbridge (Seamer)

Organists

- Olive Smith
- Harriet Gibson
- Janet Chapman

Highlights of the School Year

Anniversary Day

Chapel did not only instil in us a religious background, it also provided us with a series of character-building challenges. Probably the greatest challenge of all was the day of the Anniversary. What a splendid and heart palpitating occasion that was and the planning and preparation for it took place weeks in advance. Mr Chapman would present us all with our "pieces" to learn and practice: poetry, bible readings and songs. Every child, no matter how old, had a "piece" to learn and those children with a few more years' experience had two or three, one for each of the services held on the day: 10.30 a.m. 2.30 p.m. and 6.30 p.m. These individual "pieces" were in addition to the collective hymns and songs we sang together to celebrate the occasion.

So, preparations were a really serious part of the production and challenged and stretched the talents and abilities of each child. Woe betide you if you didn't turn up for any of the practice runs. How we rehearsed to get it right, on the day, and there was no question of forgetting. You made sure you knew it off by heart; our first valuable lesson in dedication, commitment and achieving a good standard of work. We would concentrate on our "pieces" in Sunday School, at home, back to Chapel through the week and after day school, learning, repeating, memorising. It was a real challenge not only for us but our Sunday School teachers of whom Mr. Chapman was the principal. On reflection, how he managed to fit in so many hours, on top of his every day job as a coalman, is astonishing. But he did.

Not only did our "pieces' have to be word perfect, but we were also expected to look the part and our mother would go to great lengths to ensure that her girls looked smart for the occasion, (not an easy task on a limited budget). We always had a new dress, (the only one in the year) shoes and socks. To say we felt special when we wore our new outfit is an understatement. No top model, draped in the most expensive designer creation, felt like we did on Anniversary morning. We just swelled with pride.

One year, in particular, stands out in my memory, when Mrs. Manton, the village "Bobby's wife," was called to make white satin dresses for us. Mum had returned from Farrow and Kitchings, in Stokesley, one day, with a roll of the most beautiful shimmering pure white satin material and Mrs Manton was going to make, especially for us, new Anniversary dresses. We went for regular fittings and boy, was it worth it! The finished garments were simply beautiful to us. Shimmering in the sunlight with full circle skirts that rippled and shone when you spun round; pink and blue sashes accompanying new socks and sandals. We looked a treat alongside our pudding basin haircuts.

Basil Webster took our photographs sitting on the swing in his garden at the end of the service.

To return to the moments prior to the Anniversary service itself. Breakfast was almost out of the question, so many butterflies flitting about that food was the last thing on our minds, so many last-minute questions. "Will I remember my lines?" "How many people will be there to see us?" The last was a silly question, because we knew the Chapel would be packed to capacity, full of familiar faces ready and waiting to be entertained by us. We knew, as we waited in the back room, that at any moment the door would open, a hush would fall over everyone present as we filed in, dressed in our grandeur, to climb the steps past the organ and file along to sit in the choir pews facing the congregation. Oh, how the butterflies crashed about as you looked amongst the sea of faces for Mum and Dad, Aunties and Uncles, Gran also, waiting your turn to perform. But character building it was, and, if you could get through that at 5 years old, you could face the world.

The very first initiation "piece" for all "first timers" went like this,

"I'm only a little girl (or boy),

I've never stood here before,

But if I live another year, I'll tell you something more."

No matter how many times the congregation heard those words, uttered falteringly, over the years, they always brought laughter and murmurs of appreciation, with sideways glances in the direction of that child's parents. True to say that, as we grew, and had a few anniversaries under our belts, the whole experience became more enjoyable.

Now, as we return from morning service, some fifty years later, the memories come flooding back from those formative years and, as we face those very places we occupied as children, it all seems like yesterday.

Sunday School Trip

I don't ever remember this event falling on a wet day, although I am sure there must have been times when it did. The fact is that we, as Sunday School children, were so excited at the prospect of a day away at the sea-side, that we made our own sunshine and it wouldn't have mattered what the elements threw at us on this particular occasion, when members, together with parents and Sunday School teachers, all gathered at Great Broughton cross-roads to wait for Dunning's cream and green coaches from Great Ayton to come and pick them up and carry them away for the day.

The venue was usually Scarborough, although I do remember one time we went to Whitby for a change. This trip particularly sticks in my mind because it was the one time that Mum managed to persuade Dad to accompany us, he had never done so before. Unfortunately, Whitby did not seem to hold the same attraction as Scarborough and after this it was really no contest; Scarborough it was year after year.

The night before the trip, clothing for the day was set out on the chair in the bedroom.

Ankle socks, paired up correctly, and plimsolls whitened on the back doorstep ready for the big day out, our hard saved pennies tied up in a handkerchief and safely ensconced in Mum's pocket. We went to bed early, or should I say earlier, since 6 o'clock to bed was normal bedtime for us. It wouldn't make any difference on this particular evening because were far too excited to sleep. I remember in later years Mum keeping our impending day outings a secret and not letting us know until the morning of the departure. This, at least, meant that we had a good night's sleep, and she had a far easier task in preparing us for the day out.

Next morning finally arrived, breakfast hastily devoured, clothes donned and Mum's carrier packed with swimsuits, towels, picnic and the very necessary damp flannel. Watching through the front kitchen window, we saw the first of our Sunday School comrades, with parent (s), making their way to the cross-roads and panic would start to set in, the stomach fluttering and heart beating faster, "Hurry up, they're going down, we might miss the bus - hurry up!" It was like letting out a frisky horse into the fields for the first time in the year after a long winter internment. We simply couldn't get to the cross-roads fast enough and it finally took a swift cuff across the ear, from Mum, to settle us down sufficiently in order to safely herd us down there where other over-excited children, with clucking parents, waited. The time was approximately 8.30 a.m. and all eyes would be focused on the road from Great Ayton, waiting in huge anticipation for Dunning's coaches (generally two) to appear around the bend. "Here they come!" the chorus would go up, and everyone would prepare to board.

Great Broughton was a small village community, and

everyone knew everyone, so friends would take this opportunity to sit together and gossip, catch up on the news and generally exchange chat about their everyday problems, events and forthcoming marriages, christenings etc. The comradeship of this, the most sociable event of the Sunday School year, was tangible. Most seats on the coach were occupied by the children of the Sunday School and their parents, but any spare seats would have been taken, at a modest cost, by any other person from the local villages who just fancied a day out. I can remember folk simply turning up on the morning in the hope of a spare seat and usually there was one. Children were allowed to sit together as long as they behaved themselves.

Ground rules had already been established before whitened plimsolls set foot on the bus; "No putting feet on seats, or against the rear of the seat in front. All chatter was to be kept at an acceptable level and no wandering about." Mum might be sitting next to her offspring, but a sharp cuff across the ear or stern reprimand from the nearest adult, related or not, would very soon reminding the recipient that he or she was being closely monitored and that the boundary between what was considered to be acceptable, and unacceptable behaviour, had just been crossed. Excited we might have been, but also closely controlled.

The coaches would take about two hours to get to Scarborough, passing through miles of beautiful North Yorkshire countryside. Up Hasty Bank with much grating of gears and for me the fear always that we might have to get out and push, on to the next bank Newgate, through Helmsley, Pickering and finally, after what seemed to be an interminable journey to the youngsters on board, the cry would go up, "Look I can see the sea!" Chatter would subside for a moment whilst everyone strained to catch a glimpse of the distant grey blue horizon of the sea before it disappeared at the next corner. We knew then that there was only a short distance to go and we would finally be there.

As the coach manoeuvred its way through the coach park, to it allocated parking place, Mrs. Dunning would rise from her front piloting seat and turn and face the sea of expectant faces.

"Now everybody, can I have your attention? If anyone would like to leave any possessions behind, on the coach, you are welcome to do so, but please remember that the coach will be locked until 3 o' clock so don't leave anything behind if you are going to need it. We will be leaving here at 4 o' clock sharp to be home for about 6 o' clock. Now I'll do a head count, then we'll know if we have lost anybody on our return. Have a good day out. Don't spend all your money, and kids don't make yourselves feel sick with too much rock and candyfloss. Mind the step as you get off."

A low murmur and giggles followed these instructions as one by one folk and their children in an orderly fashion, never pushing or trying to be first, alighted and gradually made their way in various directions around Scarborough.

Mum would always start our day wisely, with a trawl around Woolworths and then the open canopied street stalls which to a child's eye were magic castles laden in every colour imaginable. Plain colours and striped and all with the lettering 'Scarborough" running their full length.

There were sugar dummies, sized for a gargantuan mouth, round flat candy lollipops with smiling faces iced upon them, bacon and egg on a plate, pears, apples, bananas, strawberries, whole fruit baskets all in yummy rock candy. On the pavement outside the canopied stalls was the man, or woman, with the pinny on, working hard at a transparent revolving tub into which periodically he or she would pour pink strands of sugar candyfloss. The taste and smell of that sticky mass, to this day, still evokes wonderful childhood memories for me.

I remember one trip having saved a whole 4s 6p (equivalent to about 23p in decimal currency) I spent a whole shilling on a lovely little jewellery box covered in various shapes and sizes of shell. It stayed on my dressing table for years, and, as the little shells sometimes fell off, I would stick them back using Mum's time-honoured means of sticking broken things back together again - buy a packet of chewing gum, enjoy a good chew until all the peppermint flavouring had disappeared, then use the gum to stick one broken part to the other. In time the gum would dry out and become hard. It was a very cheap and effective way of mending broken objects, but you had to remember not to use warm water to wash the object at a later date or you would end up with the broken part again and softened chewing gum stretching in sticky gooey elastic lengths everywhere.

Happy, spending over, money no longer "burning a hole in our pockets," it was now time for the next event on our day's agenda and that was down to the beach. Mum's carrier bag would be unpacked, and we would quickly change into our swimsuits. It was the only time that we undressed in public, so modesty even at the tender ages of 5 and 8, was protected with a towel wrapped around us. A succession of quick contortions, under the towel, and we would emerge two minutes later with swimsuit on. Racing down to the waves, "Last one in's a sissy!" we were never quite prepared for the impact of the cold North Sea; bracing to say the least. It took your breath away and twelve months away had blunted rather the memory of the previous year's dip. Two minutes in there, goose bumps all over, teeth chattering, the idea of being "sissy" wasn't so bad after all and we would leave the waves to find a warmer, shallower stretch of water, which had been conveniently left behind in a hollow of the beach, when the tide had turned.

Mum would spread the towels on the sand to watch us from a distance. Those same towels impregnated with sand would become like emery paper when we later had to use them to dry ourselves.

Frolicking in the sea and chases around the beach, buckets and spades and building sandcastles with little flags on, writing messages in the sand and watching the waves erode them away, donkey rides, Punch and Judy, simple sea-side fun, so different to any other kind of play, cost little but gave immense enjoyment. We were in an element which we rarely had the opportunity to enjoy, so for us it was special and brought together all the wonderful experiences that made up our Sunday School trip day.

Appetites sharpened with all the activity and we would then sit with Mum on the towels and eat our packed sandwiches of egg and sand (why is it sand simply gets everywhere?) grating and gritty between the teeth. This would be washed down with hot tea from the flask, everybody sharing the same cup, a Blue Riband to follow and a surreptitious lick on a stick of rock. This last sin always backfired on us because, having opened the rock when told not to, the ever-present sand would adhere like filings to a magnet and you paid the price for being disobedient.

Time was rolling on and we must leave the beach, half dried hair, socks and knickers full of sand, to explore the wonders of Peasholme Park. Mum never visited Scarborough somehow without fitting in this enchanting venue.

There were the swans and boats on the lake, a lovely lakeside path to walk all the way around. At certain times of the day a brass band would play lively music from the band stand, (Mum's favourite) ice-cream vans and a little tea room. I would have loved to visit it at night-time when dusk was falling because, all the little fairy lights festooned amongst the trees around the lake, were lit at that time and so turned the garden into a real fairy land with coloured bulbs reflecting in the water. It was a real wonderland for a child, for lovers and for sweethearts, paradise for the older generation, who were happy to just sit and watch. Peasholme Park had something for everyone.

I remember once, after strict instructions from Mum about leaning too far over the side, being allowed to go out on the lake in one of the many numbered paddle boats. They were not the most manoeuvrable forms of transport since you had to 'steer' using the two handles at either side of the wooden bench seat. Turning the left handle only would put the boat in a right turn, right handle only for the opposite direction, then both handles together to plough through the water in a relatively straight line. It was a thoroughly enjoyable experience, despite the resulting blisters and all too soon the voice over the loud hailer was calling "Times up, come in number 2!"

The hours sped by and, in what seemed no time at all, Mum was heading us back in the direction of the coach park. We would arrive to find the coach doors open and the first passengers already in their seats sorting the days purchases, re-arranging bags, coats and children and relating the day's highlights, and events, with their neighbours. Little by little the coach segmented load came together again.

There was a general air of a day well enjoyed, tired

parents and exhausted children happy now to settle back into their seats, relaxed, ready for the journey back home.

Mrs. Dunning stood up at the front of the bus, once again, and carried out her head count. "We're two missing, has anybody seen Gladys Jones and Brenda Smith?" Always last to return the two with the least sense of the propriety of time keeping. "Here they come, cow's tail, at last." Another head count and everyone declared aboard. Time to go home.

It had been a good day, a happy day, a day to remember, full of simple pleasure, fun and togetherness, the only day in the year for some families to enjoy time outside their daily drudge of never-ending work and to do something different.

Sunday School Trip a true holy day.

Harvest Festival

Without doubt Harvest Festival was always a favourite occasion in Chapel.

Surrounded by a hard-working farming community, we learned from a very early age that the harvest yield was a vital part of the surrounding village's prosperity and that the effects of the weather could make all the difference between making ends meet and a real financial struggle for our neighbouring farming families.

Bob Swales, who farmed White Post farm, was also a lay preacher at our chapel, a big framed, ruddy faced, no nonsense chap; the kind they call, "The salt of the earth." With a big booming voice, which I guess had been cultivated over years of bawling across fields, no one could ever complain of not hearing his address in chapel. I know I certainly felt the brunt of that voice on one occasion when I was supposed to be diligently "spud bashing" on his farm during our October Half Term from school, but instead had stopped to have a chat with my aunt who was working alongside; from half way across the field came the order, "Stop nattering, spuds wain't pick thesel's, heads down and arses up!"

Of characters such as these was our village community made up. Colourful, honest and forthright. We were, in hindsight, privileged to have been brought up with such good role models.

Children, of course, take it for granted that there is food on their plates. Even though we were on a very limited income, we never went hungry. Grandad and Dad both worked their kitchen gardens. We lived with orchards heavy with fruit in Autumn, there just for the picking. From an early age, we were involved with the gathering in of fruit and the preservation of it for the long winter months. We picked potatoes and vegetables out of the earth, got our hands dirty and our backs aching. We gathered brambles for jam and wine, sloes also. We learned the art of jam making and bottling and wine making from the fruit we gathered, free, from the trees and hedgerows. So, we grew up with a feel for nature and natural things and Chapel Harvest Festival brought all this together and taught us to be grateful.

Our chapel was transformed at Harvest Festival time. The smells and aromas of fresh fruit, vegetables and flowers, met you before you even went through the door, smells never to be forgotten, memory evoking and deeply rooted. But those smells, wonderful as they were, could never prepare you for the amazing display, a veritable feast to the eyes, that met you in the main chapel.

Every window ledge was florally festooned. Gladioli and dahlia of every colour and hue stood sentinel above ripe and rosy apples and juicy pears. Twisted corn stalks gave a backcloth to newly washed turnips, carrots and potatoes. There were cabbages as big as footballs, parsnips white and aromatic. Every fruit and vegetable that had been grown locally was represented in one form or another. There were the wild fruits from the hedgerows, brambles, rosehips, sloes and elderberry. There were pots of jam and chutneys, bottles of homemade wine. There were representatives of foreign climes also, bananas, oranges, tangerines and the never to be forgotten, pomegranate.

Then there was the main display, which took pride of place at the front. Inside the communion rail, pouring over the side of the kneeling cushions and climbing up the front to the pulpit, at the centre, always stood the plaited bread wheatsheaf, glowing golden brown and glazed. The child in me always wondered how the bread plait could possibly be made into the shape of the wheatsheaf. It still puzzles me today. Certainly, its importance was obvious, as it always took centre position.

All these wonderful things brought together, in one momentous annual gathering, to be savoured and to give thanks for, had to be seen to be believed.

An army of willing helpers, during the week, prior to the festival, had combined to produce a truly memorable spectacle and as children, we loved it. We loved the beautiful harvest hymns, and still do, our favourite of course being, "We plough the fields and scatter the good seed on the land".

Nowadays, many children never know the true source of their food. Meat is from the supermarket, and milk comes out of bottles, apples and other fruit come in plastic containers, vegetables too. Natural, freely given fruit, is left to rot on the hedgerows and ground. Land is utilised more and more for building and its true purpose is being eroded for the sake of profiteering and land developers. I wonder how much longer we can systematically destroy our mother Earth.

Christmas Party Time

The Sunday school rooms, situated to the rear of the premises, could be accessed by two entrances, either via the main church building through the door to the right of the organ, or via a narrow external pathway running between the length of the chapel and a high boundary brick wall, through the door at the end of the path.

Apart from the usual Sunday school activities, these rooms were in continual use weekdays for a variety of events. There were the Ladies Fellowship group meetings, coffee mornings to raise funds for the Chapel and other charities, jumble sales, where many a bargain could be obtained for a few pennies. We held Bible classes there and concerts with a stage erected, where members of Sunday school and Chapel could show the village their "hidden talents." Youth club for any of the village children, members of Sunday school or not.

These rooms were the venue for much of the serious

reflection on Methodism, but also for much fun and light-hearted socialising of all age groups.

There was always a distinct difference in the aura of the two parts of the Chapel. The Sunday school rooms were often noisy, bustling, chattering and vibrant. The lives and characters of each member playing off one another, learning from one another and growing with one another; a hive of activity and development. Then through the door into the main body of the Chapel, the business of the school rooms was replaced with peaceful stillness. This was a place of worship and that commanded respect and reverence. The preacher of the day would always ask for a moments quietness from the children before they went through into the main Chapel. This calmed any over exuberant behaviour before the door opened and prepared the children for the entirely different mode of behaviour expected of them when they entered.

Sunday School Christmas Party was held in the school room, also, and, apart from Anniversary Day, was the major function that took place there. It was the final celebration of the Christian year and a natural extension to the other Christmas festivities enjoyed both at day school and home.

In the week prior to the party, ladies of the Chapel and mums would be busy baking, not only for their families, but also for the Sunday school party. So much "behind the scenes" love and effort was put into making this a very special occasion for the children.

Trestle tables (one with a precarious leg) would be set up along one wall in the big school room, covered with a snow white damask linen cloth and then laden with home-baked cakes, sausage rolls, sandwiches, jellies and blancmanges; all as colourful as the variegated strands of homemade paper streamers which stretched from corner to corner above the heads; each length tied at its anchor point with red, yellow, green, and blue balloons. There were paper stars and wheels, little lanterns and glittery snowmen and angels. The Christmas tree stood in the corner, and, at its base, the crib with Mary, Joseph and baby Jesus.

Always any event held in the Sunday school rooms would be opened with a prayer. It didn't matter if it was a jumble sale or a Christmas party. The reminder that our Lord was central to any activity which took place there, was all important, we weren't allowed to forget it.

Once settled in, with coats and hats on the pegs just inside the door, the party games would begin and every adult and child, shy or not, was encouraged to take part. It was simple, wholesome fun with cart loads of laughter and good-natured joking; self-made, high-spirited hilarity with the more the merrier. Not a television, radio, or computer play station in sight.

The couple or so hours would speed by and we all looked forward to the finale, where we plunged our arms into the bran-tub, full of saw dust, to withdraw our present for Christmas from Sunday school; blue paper wrapping for boys and pink, of course, for the girls, then happily clutching our gift, an orange, apple and balloon, we would make our way home having enjoyed a thoroughly good time.

Games we used to play at Sunday school Christmas Party

Mars Bar game: Set up a table in the centre of the room with an unwrapped Mars bar on a plate with knife and fork. In a box nearby a pair of old adult's trousers, jacket, coat, hat, boots and gloves (make them as clown like as possible). Sit the children on chairs around the periphery of the room. Adult goes from one child to the next with a tray, cup and dice. The idea is to throw a 6, rush to the centre of the room, don all the clothes, including boots, then start to eat the Mars bar using only the knife and fork. Eat as much as possible before another 6 is thrown and the next child takes over. Child in the centre must stop eating the Mars bar and take off the clothing immediately another child throws a 6.

Musical Chairs: Set up a row of chairs down the centre of the room, one less than there are children to sit on them. Chairs to be alternately facing one way then the other.

Children to walk around the chairs to music. When the music stops, child finds chair to sit on. One child of course has no seat and must go "out." Keep reducing the number of chairs until there are only two left. The child left at the end with the final chair is the winner.

NB. Another version of this game can be played without chairs. It is called "Fire on the Mountain, Run! Run! Run!"

Take a partner and stand behind him. All couples put in a circle. Child standing nearest the centre of the circle opens legs, the partner gets ready to run around the outside of the circle of children. Someone shouts "Fire on the Mountain, Run! Run! Run." This is the starter's gun for the children ready to run. They run around the circle of children all standing with legs open until the call comes "Fire's out" whereupon the runners claim the nearest pair of open legs, go through and stand in front. Each time this procedure is acted out, one child is removed from the circle so leaving more runners than open legs.

Guess the Advert: Pages taken from magazines with name blotted out. Guess what name the product is? Up to fifty of these pages would be attached to the wall around the room. Each page numbered, you had to write down the name of the product against the corresponding number on your own list, being very careful that no one else could see your answer. The person with the most right answers won the prize.

Other games played

- Here We Go Gathering Nuts in May
- The Farmer Wants a Wife
- Oranges and Lemons

- I wrote a letter to my love, and on the way, I dropped it
- Cats and Mice
- Blind Man's Buff
- Forfeits

Sunday School Choruses

In addition to the traditional hymns, and psalms, that we sang with the main body of the chapel, we also learned quite a repertoire of choruses. Short, easy to learn, melodic verses, they spoke of a child's comfort and security in his knowledge of Jesus' love for him.

These choruses were often accompanied with hand action, so making them so much easier to learn and to keep in memory, so much so that I can still remember most of the words, tunes and actions that we had practiced so many times, over 50 years ago. They were a major part of our Sunday School Anniversary Day performance and brought a lot of pleasure to the adult members of the congregation also when we performed them for other special occasions in the chapel calendar.

- Running Over
- Sunshine Mountain

- ❖ Happy, Saved, Loved
- ❖ Zacchaeus
- ❖ This Little Light of Mine
- ❖ Jordan
- ❖ Joy, Joy Joy
- ❖ Jesus' Sunbeam
- ❖ Living Bread

In relating these memories, we have pondered, laughed heartily at the funny occasions and been moved to tears, as we have re visited the old times. There have been tears of happiness as we have felt the magic of our early Sunday School years and tears of gratitude for the part Sunday School played in forming, and building, the characters of the children who attended. Gratitude, also, for the discipline and structure, it gave to our lives and immense appreciation for those individuals who patiently, and steadfastly, gave of their time, and talents, in very busy work schedules to guide and teach us.

June and Margaret Phillips

Great Broughton Chapel, about 1960

Margaret and June Phillips Anniversary Day about 1960

A Portrait of My Grandfather

George Oliver Cousans, born in 1886, husband and father of 10, died in 1972, in bed, with a fag between his fingers. It is with great relief that I am able to report that he did not set himself, the bed, or indeed the house, on fire. He certainly died happy!!

Throughout my childhood I would not say that my grandfather appeared very clearly defined at all. I can vaguely remember a rather healthy complexioned, active person who loved gardening, but who was not always as gentle with his direct relations as he was with his shrubs; hence, we, as yearlings, were extremely careful what we did, and said, and more than cautious to keep to the paths or stay out of the garden completely. "Sounds interesting," you may think, so read on. I can assure you that you will be well entertained, amused maybe, but certainly enlightened.

Grandfather was the proud owner of ten children, two of whom died from pneumonia at a very early age and are buried at the graveyard near to my home. My mother was one of the "lucky" members of the family and the tales she has to tell, concerning her childhood, would make the child welfare services of today, positively cringe! It wasn't just that he had a bad temper, it was mainly that he couldn't control it, but he certainly had ample opportunity to seek an outlet for his aggression upon his wife and numerous offspring.

I can recall my sister being chased around the garden and up the fields, for being somewhat cheeky. I do believe she had called him a bugger, not a very advisable thing to say. Fast as he was, I don't think he caught her.

Grandfather was far from being poverty stricken, well certainly not after he married my Gran, he just didn't believe in spending any of his money, particularly not upon such encumbrances as his family. When he died, his electricity bill was two shillings; he sat in the dark, no lights on, only the light from the fire to show the way. He had also stopped listening to his wireless, too expensive!

I also have vivid memories of my cousin being nearly shot with an ancient gun Grandad used to suspend on a hook, attached to the ceiling, in his living room; kept there, at the ready, in case of an intruder. Of course, we were all threatened with it at one time or another. Crazy you may think, but no one dared to go too far to discover whether he was really bluffing. But my memories are nothing compared to what my mother's must have been, and, indeed, all of her family.

"Your Grandad never did a stroke of work in his life," is the phrase which lingers in my mind from my mother's words, and, indeed, I can believe it. His passion was gardening and, from leaving school at the age of thirteen, or thereabouts, he never changed his vocation, apart from getting married and having a family. I believe, at one point, he drove a horse and trap, to market, to sell dairy products, fresh vegetables and, of course, the rabbits he had trapped. He loved a rabbit and pigeon pie!!

My Grandmother, however, came from a rather wealthy family, and, when they married, my grandfather automatically came into a bit of money. They lived in a rather gorgeous, old house with beautiful gardens and fields stretching right up to the base of The Cleveland Hills; an ideal spot for Hide and Seek and sessions of exploration, in fact, a paradise for a little girl like me.

It was in the orchard that Granny, later in her life, was to experience a very bad fall, resulting in a fracture to her hip eventually leading to pneumonia which caused her early demise, leaving George Oliver to cope as best he could.

Meanwhile, life continued in Blue Hall, for that was the name of the house, and each day exposed new, and troublesome, problems for Granny, prior to her death, to cope with. The fact was that Grandfather didn't give her any money to raise her children with, so, constantly, my mother was being sent to the bank, with a note, to make yet another withdrawal and Granny's account gradually diminished. However, it did serve its purpose in supporting the children until they could work and support themselves.

My mother left home at the age of fourteen, relieved to be free of rather a brutal father in many respects, but fearing the worst for her Mother to whom she was very strongly attached. She left with such memories of her sister being ill-treated, for sleeping in late (for Grandad was a very strong disciplinarian) and numerous other occurrences which I don't really care to describe: let it suffice the reader to know that they were too bad to print at all!

None of this really affected me in my youth. I learned to enjoy the adventures amongst the bushes and up the apple trees, in the orchard, without being too conspicuous and I learned, also, that when Grandfather demanded something, I did it, jumping to attention, no questions asked. Even, as a child, though, it puzzled me why Granny counted every penny and why, when at mealtimes, Granny's food was on the opposite side of the table to Grandfather's. Something to do with rationing after the war, I think. Very different times. When

I think about this now, it troubles me how anybody could have been so hard hearted and in fact, downright cruel, to somebody he supposedly loved, let alone had ten children to, and, as I ponder, I still think I definitely dislike him for it.

As years pass by, and age creeps on, tempers become less fiery and memories become more deeply engraved. I fear to think exactly what my grandfather thinks of his behaviour during his younger days. He is left alone, now, with no children, or faithful wife, to keep in order. The house is pretty much the same but rather worse for wear, in fact I feel rather moved to describe it to you. I feel it warrants a bit of waffling. I hope the reader will bear with me as I continue.

Blue Hall was wonderful to me, when I was small, but is equally beautiful now, although, to some, it would be the most unattractive place imaginable. It possesses no fitted carpets but, instead, plain pieces of Coco matting, especially designed to collect the dust. The chairs are cumbersome and pretty ancient, worn in places but so comfortable to curl up in. The fireplace is an antique in itself; dreadful to clean with being black lead and Grandad would dutifully get down on his hands, and knees, not easy as he aged, to clean and polish it, daily. The hearth houses a copper kettle (which continues to shine, in spite of the dust!) and a Goffering Iron which the ladies used to crimp their long dresses many years ago.

Of course, a room like this, would never be complete without its piano; a beautiful, old, polished piano with the characteristic antique clock ticking away on top. (I'm still convinced there is a mouse's nest tucked away in the back of it, judging by some of the weird scratchings which emerge, every now and again.)

The pictures, on the walls, are really lovely. They portray picturesque, olde-worlde designed houses with low, thatched rooves and multitudes of flowers festooning the fronts, a palette of brilliant colour.

The table, and chairs, are still the same as they ever were, except that a constant food supply is left out to save time, and effort, in preparing meals.

The house, itself, does not possess a water supply, and water must still be carried in a bucket from a well (you could never believe that this still exists probably, but let me assure you that it does, and Grandfather would never have it any other way.) This is his way of living and, nothing, nor nobody, will change his ideas. Very stubborn!! He is always right.

Just outside the back door there is a narrow path leading to Granny's garden, for this is what we always recognised it as. It is only very small but possesses a sort of magic air which is characteristic of this alone and cannot be found anywhere else in the remainder of the garden. Even now, I can go and sit there and sense Granny's presence. In the Summer there are thousands of beautiful flowers: roses, lupins, poppies and honeysuckle to name but a few, and in the Winter, tiny snowdrop heads can be seen peeping through the undergrowth. In the centre of the garden is an interesting, aged garden seat made of an iron bed stead head, as a back rest, and lengths of wood, nailed together, to sit on, my grandfather's masterpiece, I think. It served its purpose and didn't cost a penny!!

When you encounter a particular perfume, it is often to associate it with an occasion, person or place and this is the case with this particular garden. The association, I hold, is between the aroma of honeysuckle and the archway leading into the garden. When flowering, this smell permeates, and spreads, everywhere intermingling with sweet pea. But this is leading me away from my primary aim, in writing, and that is to describe George Oliver.

You may suppose that none of his family would want very much to do with him, but you would be wrong. Old people become less sure, both physically and mentally, and they require someone to lean upon, especially if illness strikes.

I have many Aunties, at home, and all of them help to look after him and even now, at ages ranging from forty to sixty, they still fear him a little, or so it seems. Maybe it is just a thought, but Grandfather's domineering nature never left him and he sometimes he forgets and tries to assert his authority.

I feel that it is quite remarkable what age does to people because, now Grandad is no longer so volatile in temperament, as he used to be, and, if anything, he is a little more tolerant, and respectful, towards others. Surprisingly enough we get on extremely well and have done for quite a while now, in fact ever since Granny died. What binds us together, mostly, is the old piano. It all began when I decided to try my rather limited skills on the instrument and, as Grandad sang some of the old songs, I picked up the tunes by ear and reproduced them as best I could on the keys. With a bit of practice, we progressed extremely successfully: Little Brown Jug, Danny Boy, The Blue Danube. and, of course, Christmas carols. If I close my eyes, I can still hear him warbling, at the top of his voice, reaching those high notes in his own inimitable way. Granny, however, would have turned in her grave, having never let anyone near her piano!!

It seemed that I was to become very involved, in my later life, with him, visiting regularly, for a chat about what had happened sixty years ago and I especially took sanctuary, within the garden, to revise for my exams, or, if it was too cold, outdoors, I did my revision on a rather wobbly, worn card table in front of a roaring fire. In spite of never having taken any exams, himself, he had a wonderful empathy with those who did, and an almost intellectual insight into the drawbacks of noise affecting a person who was trying to absorb knowledge. Not a word would be exchanged, when I had my pen in hand, in fact, his presence, in the opposite chair, would hardly have been noticeable, had it not been for the intermittent little grunts of content which would reassure me that Grandad was still alive and breathing, even if only in a half state of consciousness!

The time came when old age got the better of a strong will, and spirit, to continue in life, as he always had done. No longer could he seek pleasure in gardening because he simply could not bend and his gorgeous garden suffered painfully as a result, and all those, including me, who were so used to seeing well-trimmed hedges and an almost immaculate array of vegetation, and blooms, were acutely aware of the changes. He became rather poorly, to say the least, about two years ago, with cancer, and the doctor gave little hope for him. Evidently, we were informed, this growth had been with him for some time, but only on certain occasions did it really become evident and inflamed. The strong will triumphed, yet again and Grandad made a recovery.

Grandfather is still going strong, so to speak, and, judging by his appearance, he will be for some time to come. The black hair is still very dark in colour, not sure if the black boot polish has been used on it, and the complexion wonderfully clear and fresh. Only really can one hazard a guess at his true age by examining his hands. Whenever I look at them, I always remember a poem I once read entitled, "An Old Man's Hands. "It describes how the knuckles are smooth, bare and worn and the veins protrude, with age; the skin is speckled and discoloured, with old wounds, and I always visualise Grandad's hands and think of the two World Wars they fought in and the memories they must hold in their grasp and how he worked with the War Horses in World War Two. What pain he must have felt as they were slaughtered.

In spite of what he did, in his youth, and what people say about him, he is, and always will be a very special person to me and I hope that, when I return home, in my holidays, either from College or my work as a teacher, I will always be able to return to Blue Hall and find him sitting on his garden seat or in front of his big, cosy, roaring fire.

This account was written when I was twenty, fifty-two years ago, for my English lecturer, Mr. Whittaker. He gave me a Grade A for it and suggested that I could, "Return to this portrait and build it up in later years."

I have done just that.

George Oliver Cousans, Blue Hall Gardens

Jim

It was the unpredictability, of it all, that was so damaging to a small child, growing up in an aggressive, sometimes violent family.

Would he come home, from the pub, in a silly, stupid frame of mind, being the worse for drink, or would he display the behaviour we all dreaded? Argumentative, obnoxious, unreasonable, looking for a fight, bleary eyed and slurring. Not that he drank heavily, he just couldn't "hold" his drink.

I don't actually recall much detail of my younger years. I think I blocked it out, my mechanism for survival. I do, however, remember a few explosive situations that occurred.

One was when I found myself kneeling beside my mother's bed, as a small child, and she was crying. I don't recall why but am sure it would have something to do with her aggressive husband, who was also in the room.

My sister tells me, although I did not witness this myself, that my father had burned her with a cigarette end.

The occasion, that I do recall vividly, was the dark night he locked her out of the house in the back garden. We kids had to wait until he went to bed to "sleep it off" before we crept downstairs to let her back in. It had been raining.

Preventing my father going to the pub was an ongoing game for us and we regularly hid his shoes so that he had nothing to wear. This started off in quite a light-hearted way and he would find amusement in our efforts to deter him, but the mood quickly changed from irritation to anger and then we knew we had to watch out.

One night he actually went to the pub wearing his slippers! My mother was a party to all this subterfuge and the three of us, my sister included, derived great satisfaction from ganging up on him.

Then, of course, there was the night when he "left home" I don't recall what exactly had sparked this drastic move but he sought out his suitcase and packed it (we would gladly have helped to facilitate the procedure) and off he went, out of the front door, banging it decidedly behind him. I have no idea where he was going, as it was dark and quite late, no car, no buses running.

I don't remember how long he was gone, but he eventually returned to unpack and continue as if nothing had happened. I wonder now if his intention had been to go to his elderly mother, my Grandma, who lived at Windlestone, County Durham. A bit tricky travelling there at that time of night!

He had a number of sayings that he would come out with and, as I grew up, found them to be very irritating. One was, "You only pass this way once." If he truly believed this, I wondered why he hadn't made a better job of this one and only attempt. Another, and most annoying of all, "I don't keep dogs and bark myself!" I detested this one because it summed up exactly how he felt about his family.

My father's life had been a very hard one and this moulded him into the person he was, very volatile, violent, aggressive, sadistic to some extent and totally unable to demonstrate love. As the only surviving child, he was beaten by my grandma, sometimes sleeping under the hedge rather than return home. She, in turn, had been beaten by my grandfather, William, a tough Durham miner, who also drank, miners did, heavily, resulting in her "losing' a number of babies in pregnancy.

Leaving school, at a young age, my father was sent down the mine to work. No alternative, no choice. He would probably be 14 or15 at this time.

When WW2 broke out, he found himself supporting the Medical Corps, no doubt witnessing the worst of war experiences, retrieving limbs from the battlefield and trying to repair broken bodies. He never spoke of his war time exploits, only to his mates at The British Legion Club, over a pint. They understood.

After the war he returned home suffering from terrible shell shock, unable to settle into domestic life with his wife and young son. If PTSD had been recognised then, and he had been able to access counselling, our family life might have been quite a different matter.

I say that he did not know how to love, and he didn't, he had never experienced affection as a child, and none of it was his fault. On reflection, however, I just wish he could have appreciated, and valued what he had later on in life, a loving and wonderful wife who took care of him and his children. Without her, certainly, we kids would have been taken into care.

As I grew up, I coped less and less well with his destructive behaviour and, as a teenager, just before I left home to go to college, I recall an almighty bust up which my maternal Grandfather witnessed. He had returned home, the worse for wear, and slotted into his usual goading, provocative mode which, on this occasion, made me see red. I exploded at him and how he didn't "go for me' I'll never know. I think he was just too shocked at my outburst. I had had enough and let him have my wrath full pelt! I declared my hate for him and that I would never return home to see him, only to visit my mother. My poor grandparent burst into tears at the furore and quoted from the Bible, "Honour thy father and thy mother.' How could I when I had a father who, in my eyes, deserved no respect.

The day I left to go to college my mother had to remind me to say goodbye to him. "Don't cut him out altogether," she said. The fact was that he had almost destroyed me and my family. He was certainly nothing like my friends' fathers who were "normal'. I longed for a normal father, but it wasn't to be. The day I went to college I left it all behind me and started a new life.

His funeral was a strange affair because, neither my mother, sister nor myself knew what to feel. True to say I felt nothing, certainly no grief. My mother shed not a tear. We had a problem trying to think what to write on his wreath because, all the usual words people choose, for loved ones, sounded hollow. Certainly, we couldn't use "In Loving Memory" because the memories he left behind were awful.

We set off, behind the hearse and proceeded to the church where the vicar was nowhere to be found and had to be searched out, leaving us loitering at the Lychgate with the coffin containing my father. It felt like a sketch from the Dave Allan series. En route we passed the pub that had, ironically, contributed to the extensive damage to everyone in our family. The whole experience had left me numb and emotionless.

He had gone.

Damaged Daughters

She watched.
She stood and watched.
And listened to

Her sister's distraught cries.

She stood in the bedroom doorway
And watched the aftermath.

Her sister had cheeked him
And run upstairs to escape.
He pursued her to the bed.

He beat her
And wouldn't stop

She stood in the doorway
Screaming
Screaming for him to stop.
He didn't stop.

At the uproar
Mother dashed upstairs,
Restrained him.
Finally he stopped.

She watched, shaking and sobbing.
Her sister had wet herself in her distress.
Mother had saved the day, and the daughter
From what might have been done
And could never be undone.
The unspeakable.
The unmentionable.

She watched
Damaged.

Laying Those Ghosts to Rest

It was the drink that did it!
Always the drink,
That turned and turned about
the thinking and reasoning.

The night we nearly died,
my mother and me,
for ever etched in my mind,
never completely erased.

We awoke to the cloying smell
of smoke
coming from somewhere down below.

A death trap cottage was our abode.
Electric wires fizzed and buzzed.
So outdated were they.
The landlord did not care.
For six shillings a week,
no money to repair.

He had come home, worse for wear.
Boiled the kettle!
Retired to bed!
Forgot to switch it off!
Kettle boiled dry!
Ignited aged wires!
Which stretched to the ceiling.
Wooden beams ready to carry
the flames
up to sleepers above.

Miracle!
It stopped!
Fire fizzled out.

She was there.
My Guardian Angel.

On viewing the damage,
we set to work.
Scrubbing and scaling the blackness
off everything.

Cooker, sink, cupboards, curtains, walls, table, chairs.
The list was endless.
Hour upon hour we scrubbed
and cleaned.
Largely to no avail.
Little impact.

Culprit brought to face the damage.
Hardly registered.
Mute.
Returned to bed.

Next morning,
Not a mention
that we had nearly died.
My blessed mother and me.

Bessie

I always dreaded the time when my mother, Bessie, would no longer recognise me, and, sadly, that time arrived when she was in her late eighties and was suffering from Dementia. It is true that you lose your loved ones twice, once through the illness and then again when they die.

My blessed, and beautiful, Mother, inside and out, deserved a much happier life than the one that was allotted to her.

Life would not have been easy in her childhood, being one of ten children. Her education was limited and, at the age of fourteen, she left school and went in to "service" as indeed lots of young girls did. This was all that was on offer to them, particularly village girls, and meant that they would be very young when they left home and "lived in" at the place of work. It would be the norm at that time, (around the 1930's,) and very vulnerable, and innocent, girls would be prey to unscrupulous individuals out there. (Read Catherine Cookson)

My mother worked for many wealthy and influential families, one of which was for Mrs. Spencer of the original Marks and Spencer empire. Later, she cleaned, and cared for, the Sparks' Bakery family. I remember having a conducted tour of one of their factories, as a little girl, and being plied with lots of chocolate goodies, and, in particular, a wonderfully decorated Easter egg with sugar flowers and bunnies on the side. Such luxury!

The last people she cared for were the Pain's, who lived at Glenside, Great Broughton. Jack Pain worked for Dorman Long and held a key role in the construction of the Humber Bridge and the Sydney Harbour Bridge. Lovely people who really appreciated what Mum did for them. I believe, his wife, Joyce, was one of the first women to study Science at Oxford University.

During WW2 Bessie worked in Scarborough, at Rowntree's' and, it was there, we are led to believe, she met a young man, and my half-brother was the result of that relationship. She would never speak of him and only shared his name, with her son, just before she died. She was abandoned and left to cope as best she could. Very hard.

In her selfless way, she protected her daughters from her "shame" and we did not discover the truth until I was 28 and had just given birth to my little son, Peter. I could certainly appreciate then what it must have been like to part with a child, as I cradled my own.

Later she would meet my father, at Burniston Barracks, where he was stationed during the war. Big mistake!

In spite of her hard life my mother was one of the kindest, and most caring, people I have ever known. Materially she had very little, but always shared what she had. Our neighbours were well looked after: Mr. Fred Smith with breakfast in bed every morning and Tom Beynon, our neighbour at the other side, who was equally well attended to. She also cooked, and cleaned, for my grandfather, in addition to everything she was required to do to support her own family. A real hard worker who passed on her work ethic to me certainly.

I would be very young when travellers, tinkers, knife sharpeners and rag and bone men called. They all received the same welcome: a cup of tea (often in their own tin mugs which they magicked out of nowhere) and a bacon sandwich. She judged nobody but accepted them as they were. A true Christian! They would sit, in our tiny front room, sharing tales and, one lady, in particular, Mrs Adams, who had a very weathered face and, a long, black plait which hung right down her back, would arrive with a huge, wicker basket, covered with a tea towel, full of the most amazing items, for sale, for a few pence. There would be: pieces of ribbon and lace, clothes pegs, dusters, dish cloths, clothes lines, chamois leathers to clean the windows, embroidered handkerchiefs, little ornaments, lucky charms, pieces of lucky heather (no doubt collected from the moors) and so on. I would peer in to this treasure trove, deciding what I wanted Mum to buy and, true to form, she would always buy "a little bit of something" to "help out."

One gypsy lady, who hadn't called before, wasn't quite so nice! I think it must have been when Mum was a bit "hard up" which she frequently was, so she did not answer the door. The lady came to the window, peered in as best she could, the net curtains interfering with her view, and hammered on the glass, issuing expletives as she did so. Eventually, much to our relief, she left, but we were very concerned that she had put an evil spell on us!

Mum absolutely loved a Jumble Sale and saw it as a good way to top up her family's wardrobe. The said sales took place in the Village Hall and were very well supported, particularly by the people of Stokesley who would arrive, in droves, on the bus. The Broughtonian ladies knew that it was imperative that they had a good sort out of the items they wanted before the bus arrived!! Mum, in particular, loved to be "up on the stage" selling curtains, bedding and household goods. She got more pleasure from good, second-hand items than she ever would paying full price for something in a shop. She loved a real bargain.

Without Bessie to protect us, our lives would have been very different, and, I am convinced, we would have ended up in Care. She was always there for me, particularly when my babies were born. She would visit to lend support, for two weeks, no longer in case she was seen to be intruding, then she would leave, and you had to "get on with it". Her wisdom, and advice were second to none. She knew all about feeding, winding, nappy changing, Dinnifords, turning the baby over in the crib or raising it to your shoulder and why it was crying. She knew about cooled, boiled water for stomach cramps and colic and, best of all, she was there for the night feeds, offering a cup of tea at two in the morning. She was a brick, and, to this day, I shall ever be grateful for what she did for me. So full of good, common sense, support and love.

BESSIE PHILLIPS

22.05.1916 - 22. 03 2007

My sister and I sat with her in the Care Home, as she

slowly passed away. I miss her greatly but know she is still with me and have felt that presence in our family's challenge over the last five years, our eldest son's battle with blood cancer. She supports me and keeps me strong.

Thanks Mum.

Bessie Phillips, probably aged 23

"Every troubled
youngster needs a
Lizzie to escape to when
home life is so
challenging."

Jill Robinson, Published Author Of Berringden Books

Lizzie

Let me take you to my sanctuary, my bolt hole when things "hotted up" at home.

A short distance, up the High Street, heading towards the Cleveland Hills, there, on the left, take a turn in and continue up the drive to Garden House where my dear friend, Lizzie, lived.

Pass the pump, on the right, which always fascinated me, because it actually worked, and, if you pumped hard enough, clear water flowed out. I believe it was one of the two functioning pumps which served the village many years ago, when Great Broughton was still a village and not a small town.

I digress. Pass through the farm gate and there you are, you've arrived.

Garden House stands on your right with extensive fruit, flower and vegetable plots at the front. Fields stretched endlessly behind. As Lizzie was unable to tend her garden, due to old age, a neighbour, Mr. Mercer, took control. There was also a wonderful orchard, brim full of apples, pears, plums and damsons; a veritable feast.

I loved this place and its *occupant*, spending many happy

hours with my friend.

If I ever visited after dark, her back door would always be locked and I would hear a muffled voice, from within, shouting "Who's there?" before opening the door and admitting me. Then we would sit, in front of a roaring coal fire, chatting, drinking cups of tea and eating her delicious apple pie, cakes and jam tarts. Sometimes we would play games, one of which, was my favourite. Working through the alphabet you had to think of a name for: a country, a town, a river, a boy's name, a girl's name, a flower, an animal, a bird, a food item and so on. By the time you had progressed from A to Z, your brain would be buzzing!

Outside, on a warm summer's day, we would sit on her garden seat and catch up. Occasionally we would walk down her fields towards the big hay barn. But there lay a dark secret, which, as a little girl, disturbed me alarmingly.

There were always legions of cats around, many wild and feral, and, as cats do, they caught mice and rats, all well and good you might say, but they also produced lots of offspring. The big shed was where they made their nests, snuggled amongst the hay and straw, lovely and cosy and warm, and had their babies. Quite safe to raise your brood you would think, but not when Lizzie was on the prowl! She had to control the numbers and her way of doing it was to put the kittens in a bucket of water, in her Wash House, with a lid on. She saw absolutely nothing wrong with this method. Even now, as I think about it, I feel a bit sick and squeamish. Different times, different goings on!

My friend was a staunch Methodist, and we would go, together, to the evening service, warble to our heart's content and listen to the sermons, some of which were full of fire and brimstone and kept you totally engaged, frightening me to death with talk of hell and damnation. Others were not quite so soul stirring and left you feeling a bit soporific.

Lizzie, sadly passed away, when I was 23 and at college. I knew that she hadn't been well for a while, and I had visited her in hospital. But, on returning home, one day, I was told that she had died, which was heart breaking for me. Prior to receiving the sad news, I had been to her house and had wandered around outside, gazing through the windows, and hoping to speak to her, wondering where she could be, but fearing the worst. The house was forlorn, and her spirit was gone.

She died the year I was married which upset me greatly as I would have loved for her to be there. After the wedding, I took my bouquet and laid it on her grave, the best thing I could think of to do.

Her funeral was at Great Broughton Methodist Chapel, which no longer exists, and was a beautiful service. My mother sat with me, in Chapel, as I couldn't control the tears. I felt utterly bereft. She left a big, black hole in my life. She had been a true friend and I loved her.

It is sometimes the custom, in villages, to sell the possessions of the deceased in the Village Hall. I was anxious to keep something belonging to Lizzie, that I could treasure, and I had always admired a China prayer book which took pride of place on her sitting room mantlepiece. As I couldn't be present for the sale, Mum bought it for me, and I still have it 50 years later.

A wonderful memory of a wonderful lady.

Lizzie Baimbridge's porcelain prayer book, which I was bought in the sale of her possessions in The Village Hall, Great Broughton.

For Lizzie

She was my secret sanctuary,
A safe haven in which to hide.
From the "Brooding Black Cloud"
Ever there I could abide.

She knew my piteous plight,
Provided refuge for me there.
I loved her very dearly,
But needed to beware.

Why?

Because she left me.
Journeyed to a "better place."
Too ill to remain here.
Gone on, not a trace.

Of her left behind.
But wait, what's this?
A China Lord's prayer book,

Reminds me of her and what I miss.

Those times we had together:
Sunday lunch and lemonade,
Warm welcome at the back door,
Once there, I could have stayed

For ever.

Those times we prayed together.
Sunday chapel, Sunday night.
In the little village,
Great Broughton, it felt so right

To be with her in times of trouble.
A safe haven in which to hide
From the "Brooding Black Cloud"
Ever there I should abide.

Home baking: scones and cakes,
Apple pie and coconut slice.
Cups of tea at any time,
Disappeared in a trice.

"Garden House" with village pump.
Kitchen garden, produce piles,
Apple orchard, be-jewelled trees
Fields that stretched for miles and miles.

Wash house with its deadly secret,
Lids placed firmly overhead
Drowning kittens in a bucket
Certainty they're really dead.

Sad to say she could not stay
To witness my white wedding day.
Bouquet of flowers I embraced
I lay upon her resting place.

She was my secret sanctuary,
A safe haven in which to hide,
From the "Brooding Black Cloud"
Ever there in my heart abides.

Granny Cousans

Cecelia Mary Cousans was an only child, unusual in those days when families were large, child mortality was expected and accepted.

Born on 10th July 1884, she died, at the age of 80 on 15th September 1964 when I was 14 years old, from a fall in the orchard, which resulted in pneumonia.

I recall, vividly, her funeral at Kirby in Cleveland. The family assembled around the open grave, on a cold, grey day. Crows were noisily making their presence felt, up in the treetops and I stood with the rest gazing down on the coffin, the inscription clearly legible on the top.

Suddenly, my Aunty Mary, who was very close to her mother, tried to climb down into the grave and had to be restrained.

What memories for a young girl of 14. Absolutely awful. This experience has made me adamant that there will be no children at my funeral.

Cecelia was the daughter of William and Elizabeth Chappelow, the former being Stationmaster at Great Ayton for 30 years (a job with status, earning respect in the community), Elizabeth was a skilled seamstress.

Cecelia's downfall was that she met, and married, my feckless grandfather, who gave her 10 children, her only respite from child bearing being during the years of 1916 to 1920 when George Oliver was away at war. Two of her babies, George William and William Chappelow Cousans died of pneumonia in 1911 and 1912 aged 9 months and 18 months. What an absolute shock from being an only child to being the mother of 10 and then losing 2.

The ancient, spacious house that they lived in, Blue Hall, was damp and extremely cold, not conducive to rearing healthy offspring.

Grandad would relate the painful occasion, when Granny was sitting in her chair, in the front room, next to the window and aspidistra, nursing her little boy, silent tears streaming down her face. She had lost him, he died in her arms and there was nothing she could do.

The 14 years, in which I knew my Granny, left me with many memories filled with admiration and amazement at her strength in coping with it all.

My Grandfather was not exactly the most effective bread winner and Granny often had to dip into her reserves to maintain a reasonable family life. When her parents had died, within a short space of each other, one from a broken heart, she inherited a substantial amount of money, enabling her to buy the Blue Hall Estate comprising of the house itself, fields, orchards, out buildings and amazing gardens.

Years later she was to be pressured to sell it all by a very stupid , naive husband, who did not appreciate its true value, and a scheming neighbour who had his sights set on acquiring it, by whatever means he could, having walked his dogs across the fields, with my Grandparents' permission. It went out of the Cousans' family for "a song", but, I am happy to say, not without cost to the family who acquired it. The wife declared that the Cousans' Curse had been cast on them, and, indeed, it did seem that way. One of their sons died young of cancer, the father suffered ill health and then his business went bust. Retribution indeed.

My poor Grandmother never recovered from its sale and cried for days afterwards. It must have counted for one of the major scandals of the village at that time.

When I was probably no older than 8, I remember her trying to teach me to crochet. She was an amazing needle woman. She could knit, sew, embroider, darn and crochet. I stood beside her, in the same chair, next to the window and aspidistra, but could I get the hang of it? I could not and she gave up in the end. Interestingly enough, years later I learned to crochet and made many lovely items which I still have. She made all the Christmas presents for her ever-expanding family: lots of knitted socks, scarves and woolly hats. Everyone got something for Christmas and birthdays.

One year, for my birthday, she gave me a box with 6 compartments and in each was a small gift: a brooch, some sweets, a pressed flower, a tiny book and a piece of embroidery. so very special and thoughtful. But, the best gift of all, was the Swiss chalet musical box, which stood on the sideboard in the Parlour, the one I had always loved, and, occasionally, been allowed to hold and wind up. When Irish Eyes Are Smiling was the tune. I like to think that Granny gave it to me because she knew I would take care of it. My Aunty Mary had given it to her in 1953 and it will eventually go to my little granddaughter, Caya, in Australia.

Smoking, at that time, was a very fashionable thing to do and both my Grandparents smoked like chimneys. Gran even had a slightly yellow tinge to the front of her grey hair, which, I was told, and I'm not altogether sure if there is any truth in this, she washed in Daz! Grandad had yellow fingers and a groove in the ones which held the cigarette. He actually died in bed with a cigarette in his hand. Goodness knows how he didn't set himself, and the bed, on fire. At least he died happy.

If there was one quality I really admired my Grandmother for, it was her strength and determination to step in when the situation demanded that someone should take control. She was a very strong woman, she had to be.

One of her daughters had committed the ultimate sin by becoming pregnant, outside marriage, and subsequently deserted by the father. The daughter needed to work and was not in a position, financially, to support her little son. The only option open to her was to put the child up for adoption. Barnardo's was mentioned. My wonderful Granny would not countenance this idea, declaring that the child was a Cousans and, consequently, must somehow remain in the family. But, how to do this without my grandfather knowing?

A cunning plan was devised to bring the child, by train, from Scarborough to Stokesley Station, where my Gran and Annie would be there to receive him. The mother, who was still producing milk, at 6 weeks old, then had to make the return journey, alone and without her baby. Can you even begin to think what that felt like? My Grandfather was led to believe that the baby was an evacuee from the city. Unfortunately, he discovered the truth and duly banned his daughter from returning home, to visit, for 2 years.

Punishment for being a "fallen woman".

The little boy grew up as my aunty's son and stayed in the village so that at least his mother remained in contact with him. He did not discover the truth, that his Aunty Bessie was in fact his true mother, until he was 15 and about to join the Navy. Very painful indeed but at least she had not lost him altogether. The details of it all were revealed to the wider family many years later.

The mother of that child was my mother and, amazingly, I had another brother.

Blue Hall

Red rose of remembrance,
Stolen from a stem.
Blue Hall, the old homestead,
Never to be ours again.

Up the ancient masonry,
Climbing, clinging on.
Silent witness over years,
To life and love, now gone.

It was the Cousans family,
Cecelia and George.
And ten of their offspring,
Two to die as babes.

Pneumonia knew no mercy,
Dampness took its toll
Buried just along the way,
At peace, at rest, as one

Red rose of remembrance,
Stolen from a stem.
Blue Hall, the old homestead,
Never to be ours again.

Delightful, distant dreams.
A childhood full of cheer.
Cottage garden filled with flowers.
A floral feast is here.

Delphiniums and roses
Honeysuckle's bloom
Lupin, also sweetpea arch
But...

Best beloved of all,
And...
Most treasured,
The simple snowdrops, standing sentinel in spring,
Like silent, solemn soldiers
Beside the well-worn path

Red rose of remembrance
Stolen from a stem
Blue Hall, the old homestead
Never to be ours again

Granny's garden's aura,
Special little place.
Garden seat, we sat upon,
Filled with peace and love and grace

Grandad's patch so different,
Knees and back he'd bend.
Carrots, peas potatoes,
Neat rows to feed and tend.

Homely comforts missing.
No toilet, water, bath
But...
Roaring fire in open range
And...
Aspidistra in its glory.
Silken, shiny-leaved.

Red rose of remembrance,
Stolen from a stem
Blue Hall the old homestead,
Never to be ours again.

Proud piano, lid closed,
Parlour hardly used.
Weddings, christenings, funerals,
Family gatherings too.

And on that proud piano,
Standing strong and square,
The clock, its tick spoke clearly,
Amid the silence there.

Not a single sound
Therein could be heard,
To mar that magic moment
Never to be disturbed.

Orchards filled with apples,
Sledging fields of fun.
Stretching to the hillside,
No more, all is gone!

Red rose of remembrance,
Stolen from a stem,
Blue Hall, the old homestead,
Surely to be ours again.

Blue Hall Revisited

Blue Hall, The Holme, Great Broughton was the family home of George Oliver and Cecilia Mary Cousans, (my grandparents), for many years, and the front bedroom (facing The Wainstones) bore witness to ten home births, eight of which survived but two little boys, William and George, died of pneumonia (buried at Kirkby in Cleveland). This precious place left the family under highly questionable circumstances and was later "carved" up for maximum profit, a source of great pain, and anguish, to the Cousans' family.

On July 27th, 2021, I revisited the old homestead, after many years of absence due to my sadness at its loss (my mother feeling it even more acutely)

Claire Jones, and her lovely family, feel 'honoured' to live there and love the house, taking great care to nurture it alongside the gardens. Having now met these wonderful people, I know my grandparents would have been delighted that their precious home was left in such safe hands.

I spent two hours with Claire reliving old memories as I was given a conducted tour of the house and grounds. George and Cecilia definitely accompanied us.

I recounted my childhood memories.

The front room, now the kitchen, was the main hub of activity, accommodating a large Press, roll top desk, ancient piano, large centre table and black range fireplace. Eight children stood around the table to eat their meals, there being insufficient chairs to sit on. Granny would sit by the window, alongside the aspidistra, crocheting, knitting and embroidering (Christmas and birthday presents for everyone). There she sat and nursed her two dying babies with tears trickling down her cheeks. Tripe and onions bubbled in the pan on the open fire, tea leaves were thrown up the chimney to help clear the soot, hot tea was slurped from the saucer to cool it. When Granny was alive no one was allowed near her beloved piano, bur after her death, I learned to play "by ear", and Grandad would sing at the top of his voice: Little Brown Jug, Blue Danube, Danny Boy and Abide with Me. What a din we made, but we loved it.

As a little girl I was mesmerised as I watched Grandad shaving. Newspaper laid out, shaving soap prepared, cutthroat shaver sharpened to perfection. Up and under the chin, under and round the nose, finally cheeks. What a rigmarole, but a clean shave, and a few cuts, were the result, with bits of paper stuck on to stem the blood flow.

On through the house and up the stairs to the window, on the landing, overlooking the pea patch where June, Carol and Joan, one evening, nicked the peas and beans, filling their faces to capacity and, without their knowledge, being surveyed by Grandad at that window on the landing. We got off lightly as, in his younger days, he would have been "after us", maybe with his gun!!!!!!

Into the garden for refreshments. Granny's Garden. A seat made from an old iron bedstead and bits of wood to sit on. A garden perfumed with roses, sweetpeas, honey suckle and lupins. Magic!!!!!! A huge cottage garden tenderly tended by Grandad and full of produce, enough to sustain the family.

The old Wash House is gone but I remember it well. Cold water tap (only source of water to the house), set pot, dolly stick, posser, wringer, mangle, corrugated iron tub, Daz, Omo and Sunlight Soap. Imagine the activity on a Monday morning washing all those nappies!!! On the wall of the Wash House hung the old zinc bath.

No bathroom, no flush toilet. I don't think many baths would be taken at all and there was an "earth toilet" up the garden path (a bit tricky in the winter, hence the chamber pots under the beds.) Snow drops stood sentinel along the path to the privy, guiding the way.

Back into the house and memories of The Parlour. This was a small, but special room, saved exclusively for weddings, funerals and christenings and if someone of note came to visit. I loved this room, with its very distinctive and unmistakable smell, full of ornaments, trinkets, pictures on the walls and family photographs. But best of all, on the sideboard, stood a musical box, a little chalet type house which played "When Irish Eyes Are Smiling." Granny allowed me to carefully touch and wind it up and later she gave it to me for my birthday. It had originally been given to her by my Aunty Mary in 1952. I took it with me on my recent return visit to Blue Hall, wound it up and played it for everyone to enjoy with me. The little musical box had come home. A very poignant moment and one to stir the ancestors' spirits.

Well, I could go on, because Blue Hall and its sledging fields, ample orchards, extensive gardens, pungent pigsties and even more pungent earth toilets, the wash house and ultimately happy memories was central to my childhood, shaping the clay of my youth and I loved the place and the people in it. The place where I studied peacefully for school exams in front of the big, black, roaring range with Grandad sitting opposite me silently snoozing. The dubious way Blue Hall was lost to my family is still a source of pain, but I like to believe that one day justice will prevail and that it will be returned to my family.

I left, following my visit, with very mixed emotions and feelings and a great deal to think about but I have an invitation to return which I will definitely take advantage of. Thankyou Claire.

Granny Cousans in her garden at Blue Hall, the tea cosy on the tea pot clearly visible.

Granny Cousans with five of her ten children. My mother, Bessie, is on her lap.

Our Next Door Neighbour

When I was growing up, in Aberdeen Cottage, 70 The High Street, Great Broughton, we had a wonderful old gentleman who lived next door to us in a two up two down cottage, attached to ours. No modern facilities: cold water tap, no bathroom, semidetached wooden earth toilet, with cut up newspaper suspended on a piece of string ready to be torn off at a pertinent moment.

The gentleman, in question, was Mr. Fred Smith, a retired farmer, who lived all alone, having lost his wife years before I really became acquainted with him.

He was a kindly character who always called me Miss Junie and it was my task, every morning, to take him breakfast in bed, which consisted of a strong cup of tea, two sugars, and a plate of bread and butter, cut into triangles which my wonderful mother had prepared.

I would quietly enter his cottage, I can't remember having a key to unlock the door, so I guess it was left open all night (perhaps those were safer times) and I would cautiously climb the stairs, being careful not to spill the contents of the tea cup.

Before I reached his bedroom door, I would shout, "It's only me" so as not to alarm him if he wasn't fully awake. There he would be, propped up in bed, ready to receive what was on offer and was always so appreciative, you would think I was presenting him with a banquet!

His cottage was like ours, old Jet Miners' homes, and very basic. A front room, back kitchen and, I think, a little pantry which housed the cold tap and sink. It may have had a press, like my Granddad, to keep food in and the flies off. No fridge. A coal fire would warm the front room and that was it as far as heating went. A hot water bottle and plenty of blankets kept you warm upstairs and protected against the frost on the inside of the bedroom window, in Winter.

As the earth toilet was outside, it was essential to have a chamber pot, under the bed, if you were "caught short" during the night.

The "bin men' emptied the earth toilets' contents each week, which involved carrying it through the house, usually at breakfast time. My mother would send my sister, and I, upstairs, during the process, so as to protect our sensibilities. It didn't bother us in the least, we didn't bat an eye lid, all part of village life. At that time everyone had such facilities.

To return to the front room. On the sideboard,

prominently positioned, was a picture, in its frame, of a grandson, Peter, on his Graduation Day. Grandad was so very proud of this achievement and would refer to it frequently with great pride.

An abiding memory of Mr. Smith was his kindness in taking our family, (my Mum and sister) to the seaside. We would set off, early in the morning, in his little, black Austin and would embark on the scenic route to Whitby via Ingleby Greenhow, Kildale, Commondale, Castleton, Danby and on to Whitby. Scenic, yes, but also a bit hair raising, as this was the road that was full of steep hills and sharp bends.

I can remember sitting on the back, leather seat and wondering if this little car would ever make it up Commondale Bank. Very slowly we would wend our way along, engine labouring, in first, and us willing it on. Goodness knows what my mother was feeling in the front seat. Our driver in complete control, I think!! We would be "dropped off" at our destination for a lovely day by the seaside (if it wasn't raining) and spend our time, on the beach, having fish and chips, of course.

Mr. Smith would then drive on to Ruswarp Mart, catching up with fellow farmers, from the past and current prices of stock.

Later in the day we would meet him, in Whitby, before embarking on our return journey home.

A very good time was had by all. Happy Memories.

Our neighbour, Fred Smith, sitting at the back of Aberdeen Cottage, Great Broughton, surrounded by a profusion of geranium and trailing begonias.

Blessings

After a bit of a rocky start, in life, I have to say things drastically improved for me and I have many things to be thankful for.

- I have never gone hungry, or thirsty.
- I have always had a roof over my head.
- I had an amazing Mother who held it together.
- I have been married for 50 years and been loved and cared for.
- I have two sons who I could not be prouder of.
- Three Grandchildren make me very happy.
- I have an adopted family which has given me another little Granddaughter.
- I had a teaching career that spanned 40 years which I absolutely loved and would not have chosen to do anything different.
- I live in a beautiful house in a stunning environment and have done for the past 34 years.
- I am lucky enough to be in very good health.
- I am absolutely loving retirement, and every day is like a holiday. We try to do one "nice thing" every

day, be it meeting friends, going for a walk, having lunch, or coffee out, visiting interesting places or going on holiday.

- I am lucky enough to have amazing friends, and ex colleagues with whom I meet regularly.
- I have my faith which has sustained me through challenging times recently.

The list could go on. Suffice it to say, it worked out well in the end.

Other Ramblings

Echoes Of A Bygone Age

Eskdale Chapel

I stand, in contemplative mode, and study the ruin before me, that is known as Eskdale Chapel.

As I watch, and listen, I imagine that I can hear the echoes from distant times; singing of the well-known, and well loved, hymns; listening to the sincere tones, and sentiments, of the preachers, and all delivered with a backdrop of bleating lambs and ewes concernedly calling their young.

Thirty two years living in the Esk Valley, it has taken Coronavirus to wake me up to the fact that Eskdale Chapel exists, discovered during a desire for fresh air and exercise.

Built in 1224, and originally utilised as a Hermitage, it was subsequently used for worship between 1394 and 1764. A mere shell of the original building exists, but there are sufficient stones to demarcate the outline of the chapel, now overgrown by weeds and nettles and occupied by grazing sheep. A true Thomas Hardy scene.

Dramatically, so the story goes, a murder took place here, over a wild boar, which was being pursued by local, hunting landowners, when the said animal took sanctuary in the Hermitage. Feeling robbed of their quarry, the hunters attacked the hermit, who eventually died. Apparently, this incident led to the local tale of the planting of 'The Penny Hedge,' a tradition continued to this day.

My imagination continues to run riot as I depart from the Chapel and tackle the steep climb up to Eskdaleside. Legs aching and pace slackening, I dwell on what it must have been like for members of the congregation, young, old and possibly infirmed, who had to conquer these slopes, all in the name of religion. Whether on foot, horseback or pony and trap, it must have been a challenge, especially in winter. Sounds of those long-gone, local denizens' voices, call out to me now.

Magic moments are ever present in this place, creating a connection with nature and a wider, more profound purpose. Hopefully we will learn some valuable lessons from recent challenges and appreciate more fully what has been bestowed upon us.

Truly Blessed

And if you wonder why, then just take a look at the view from my balcony, along the Esk Valley.

At no time have I appreciated my blessings more than during this time of lock down. We are spoilt for choice when selecting our walks. How lucky. My heart goes out to those less fortunate.

Mike, and I, have lived here for thirty-two years and, were advised, when we moved to Whitby, that if we were still here after five years, we probably would never leave. How right they were. I can't imagine a more beautiful place to live.

Visitors, to our home, always wax lyrical at the view from our kitchen window.

So, Eskdale Chapel was discovered during one of our daily sojourns. Not much left to see, but it is a wonderfully atmospheric place. This has become one of our favourite walks.

TRULY BLESSED? NO DOUBT ABOUT IT.

"It's Not the Winning, It's the Taking Part"

REALLY ????

I don't usually attend football matches, in fact I can't remember the last time I went to one, apart from my most recent, and memorable, experience of attending my 9 yr. old Grandson's gathering. Memorable for the wrong reasons, it has to be said.

Grandma and Grandpa stood along the perimeter fence, watching and encouraging. Alongside were 3 dads who truly had to be heard to be believed. They were loudly shouting advice, loudly criticising their sons' moves, loudly vocalising their thoughts and opinions, of the standard of play and the referee's decision making, in particular.

Well, I have heard of this parental interference at matches before, which has sometimes ended up in fisticuffs, but actually being there was something else. I had an overwhelming urge to tell them to zip it and just let the kids enjoy playing. Being the coward I am, I didn't, BUT, I did turn to them at the end and remarked on what a very good game it had been (we won

5-0) and how the children had given of their very best.

They weren't having any of it and declared an anticipated state of depression for the rest of that Sunday. No doubt their sons would get an earful of advice and criticism, for the next time, over roast beef and Yorkshire pudding.

What happened to doing your best, working as a team and enjoying the game? These parents are destroying all of that. Perhaps they are trying to re-live their youths, successes and failures, through the next generation.

So very damaging and a great shame.

I won't be rushing to the next football match, I can tell you. No wonder some of our youngsters are so aggressive when they have role models like these to emulate.

The Mallyan Spout Hotel

We have just had a couple of days, pre - Christmas celebrations, with friends, at The Mallyan Spout Hotel in Goathland.

So, what draws us back, again and again, to this wonderful little jewel in Heartbeat country?

Is it the excellent service and wonderful staff, the quaintness of the hotel itself, the picturesque surroundings, the warm welcome received every time we go, the superb food on offer, the amazing Christmas atmosphere created by the outstanding decorations in every room, the chiming of the church clock across the road, the hooting of the owl in the tree outside the bedroom window or the moorland sheep wandering aimlessly outside?

It has got to be a combination of all these factors which create the special ingredients for this successful enterprise. We love it.

The Simple Snowdrop

Best beloved of all, and most treasured,
the simple snowdrop stands
sentinel in spring, like silent,
solemn soldiers beside the well-worn paths.

Unpredictable appearances in barren winter beds,
Unexpected encounters in woodland walks.
Cautiously appearing through dense leaf mould
and undergrowth, persevering and succeeding where others fail.

Promise of future hope and joy echoing God's rainbow pledge.
Simple snowdrop, stunning winter wonderland landscapes.
Some single stems, others a carpet of brilliant white
drooping heads slowly, and steadily, swaying in the gentle breeze.

Naughty Dottie and The Gingerbread House

Max and Seb are two of the best-behaved boys you could ever wish to meet. They are hardly ever naughty and always try to do as they are told, so that is why, what happened, in this story, was particularly unfair on them.

They had been presented with a gingerbread house each, not completely erected, oh no, the houses arrived in pieces of varying shaped ginger biscuits comprising of two roof and four wall segments, all ready to glue together with white water icing, and finally to decorate with chocolate Smarties of all different hues.

Well, when the boys clapped eyes on the kits, they couldn't wait to get started and what an amazing job they made of them.

Carefully laying out all the pieces, on the kitchen table, they began to assemble them, not an easy task. The icing needed to be meticulously mixed with just the right amount of cold water, otherwise it wouldn't work in the piping bag. Too runny would mean it wouldn't glue the pieces together, too thick and it would be impossible to squeeze through the nozzle. It has to be said that two pairs of hands were needed at various stages of the construction.

Max and Seb carefully piped around the windows and doors, also the roof tiles and when the final touches were completed, the boys stood back to admire their handiwork. Absolutely splendid to say the least. They were very pleased with themselves.

The next stage was to leave them somewhere to set without disturbance, so, as a temporary measure, the middle of the kitchen table was agreed upon.

Unfortunately, this was not really a good decision, and, given the past history of two thieving dogs, in this household, it was definitely not a good idea. (Coco, in particular, the black Labrador, had a reputation for scaling the kitchen work surfaces to steal food. Two birthday cakes had had chunks gobbled out of them in the past).

But, it wasn't Coco this time, it was the other little villain, a dachshund, Naughty Dottie who had attempted a mountaineering act up onto the bench and from there on to the kitchen table. She had been so quick, and sneaky, that the theft had only been detected when Mum came into the kitchen to discover the evidence under the table, chunks of gingerbread biscuits interspersed with Smarties and Naughty

Dottie right in the middle of it.

It was Seb's house that the thief had targeted and half the roof, with Smarties, had been gobbled up.

Naughty, Naughty Dottie. She looked very guilty, and a little bit nauseas after her feast. Happy to say she seemed to suffer no ill effects following this crime.

Poor Seb, all his good work and careful consideration, had been wrecked, but he was very brave and covered his emotion admirably.

Needless to say, there is another instalment to this story about the gingerbread houses, not involving a dog this time, but another miscreant, or should I say miscreants, beginning with M and ending in E, but you will have to wait to catch up on the next stage of the fate of the gingerbread houses.

The gingerbread houses which were subject to attack from dogs and mice!!!

Sebastian, my grandson, with Naughty Dottie the thieving Dachshund.

Stranger In Our Midst

In the flash of an eye
Thirty years have gone by
since first I felt compelled to write.
Kept it for a time, secreted it away,
Then burnt it to ashes.

Fearful it might be seen
Fearful it might cause hurt.

Had I lost him?
No longer recognised,
Felt so alienated.

Watched as he went off the rails.
Watched him led astray.
Watched as he challenged and kicked back,
like a cornered animal.
Watched him steadily slipping away.

Adolescence!!

Helpless!
Powerless!
Anxious!

What to do?

Plan of action.

Hang on in there.
Like them, love them.
Cast out the safety net, widely,
ready to catch them when they fall
And haul them back in.

Hang on in there.
Give it time
And patiently wait for that bend
in the road.
That crossroads

That tells you
All will be well.

It was.

View From My Balcony

Lone, isolated, elderly shepherd,
Stiff limbed and slow to move.
Aided by his well-worn crook.
As he tackles the gently undulating slopes
Where his sheep graze greedily
Nibbling at the winter wonderland.

It's a small, receding flock.
He, no longer fit and able.
But, he visits regularly
To top up their scant store.

They know him.
Run, bleating loudly, urgently
In anticipation.
Surround and nudge his tired, aching legs,
Obscuring his shrivelled frame, almost entirely.

They expect.
He provides.

Lone, elderly shepherd
Stumbles silently away.
They watch him go.
He'll come another day.

Bright Eyes

Beautiful baby.
Precious child.
So near and yet so far.

Infectious laugh.
Sunny smile.
Powerful personality.
Endearing, engaging.

God's precious gift.
Little Greek goddess.
Caya.

Life changer!
Enricher!
Completer!
Clue giver as to what it's all about.

A little longer we must wait,
(Be patient)

For that cuddle and closeness.
The soft, smooth, silky, skin,
To stroke, caress and kiss.

Nearly there.

All my love

Grandma xxx

January 2020

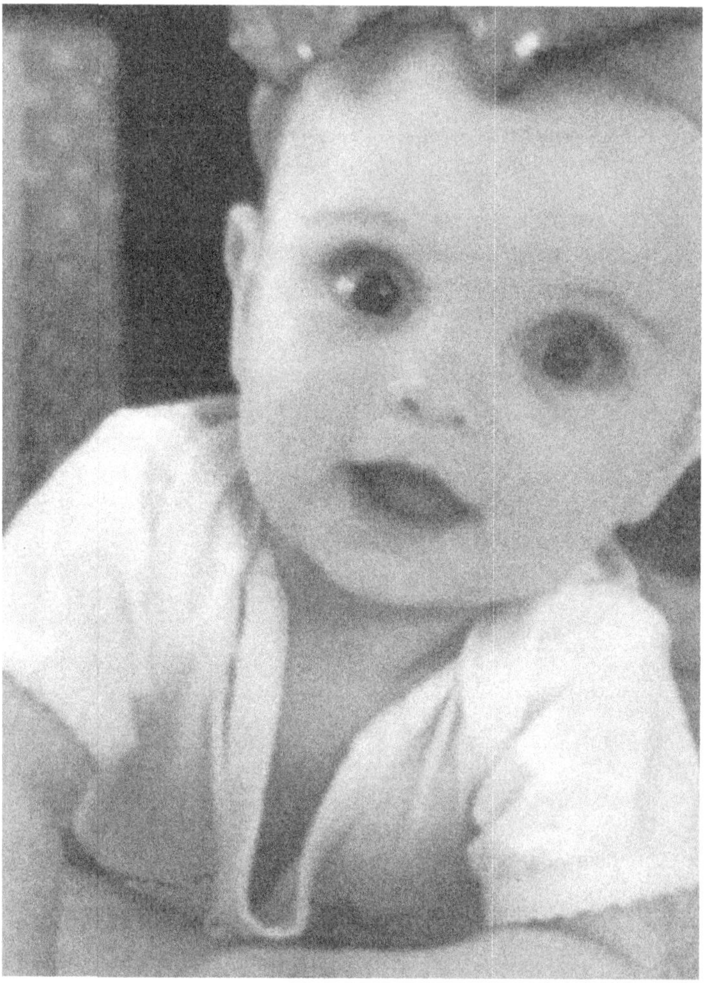

Caya, my darling little granddaughter who lives in Australia.

Musings from a Pew

Suspended from a single, silken thread.
Spinning, silently in the soft breeze.

Red Admiral Butterfly.

Dangles from the church eves,
Shadowing the stained-glass window,
As silvern shafts of sunlight penetrate the shade.

Death trap!
Spider spun
No escape!
No rescue!
Too late!

Beautiful Butterfly, Heaven Bound.

Trapped butterflies in Stokesley Methodist Church,

unable to escape.

In Flanders Fields

In Flanders Fields I stand and stare.
Mourn those who lie in earth once bare
Young lives cut short, a painful end
Brothers in Arms to the Lord we send.

Why do we never learn the lessons taught?
History repeats and all for naught.
Mourning the loss, such dreadful pain.
So many touched, and scarred, no gain.

In Flanders Fields the poppies blow
Blood red petals sway too and fro.
Black death centres a solemn, stark sight
Of futile family anguish and piteous plight.

In Flanders Fields white crosses stand
For miles and miles on disturbed land.
'It must never happen again' we're told'
But it will!

Urunga Boardwalk

Projecting far out into the sea,
Flanked on either side by Mangroves,
Generating a mosquito menace
In the sultry afternoon heat.

Swooping sea birds soar and skim.
Basking lizards rock resting
Suspiciously surveying the scene.

Behold.

A bejewelled crab family
Fit for the window display
At Boodles of Bond Street.
Sparkling sapphire blue
in the shimmering sun.
Scurrying along the smooth, sandy surface.
Popping in and out of their holey homes
and sheltered tunnels.

We do not tarry

As the midges begin to bite

Swiftly homeward bound.

Bellingen Dorrigo Urunga

September 8, 2020

The best boardwalk on the east coast. Urunga Boardwalk is 1km of spectacular views, passing along the banks of the Kalang River, to the junction with the Bellinger River and out to the ocean.

And it's wheelchair accessible the whole way.

Maroubra Beach

Ocean Observations

Watching wild, wonder-filled waves
Rearing and bucking.
Equine like.

Sea spray tossed high into the air,
Surfacing at pointed peaks,
As they curl and break.
Pulsating power.
Super surfing.
Surging towards the shore.
Carrying shells, shale,
Flotsam and jetsam.

Continuous rising and rolling.
Endless, unceasing energy.

But.
Beware!!!
Beneath the breakers

Lurks an ancient predator
Surveying its watery kingdom.
Waiting.
Waiting.

Western Escarpment walking track. Maroubra
Credit: Elinor Sheargold/DPE

Arthur Byrne Reserve, adjacent to the beach, is a large, grassed park, with barbecue facilities and picnic tables. The park also has a shaded kids' playground, impressive skate park and free outdoor gym. Jack Vanny Reserve is on the norther headland. Follow the steps down to delightful Mahon Pool, a popular rock pool where you can swim in a spectacular setting.

Mahon Pool, Maroubra

Across the road from the beach, the beautifully-restored The Bay Hotel & Diner, built in the 1920s, serves up great pub fare and is family-friendly, with a separate children's play area.

There's also the Maroubra Seals for a relaxed, bistro-style meal. The Pavilion Beachfront is located on the beach promenade itself, offering an extensive breakfast and lunch menu, along with premium ocean views.

Stroll along Marine Parade and McKeon Street for casual dining options, such as North End Café Chalk Espresso Café and Pool Café. There are more options at nearby shopping centres Pacific Square and Maroubra Junction. Head to Golden Unicorn for some of the best yum cha outside of Chinatown Kokoroya for modern Japanese food.

Stephen 50 Years Ago

Stephen sits on the icy steps.
Little sisters sit there too.
Stephen is in charge.
Dad sates his thirst within.
What time is it?
Nobody knows, least of all the drinker.
Mum long gone.

Stephen smells, at school.
Unkempt, unwashed, neglected.
Kids avoid him, especially in summer.
Sits on his own, window open.

Sometimes Stephen has bruises.
Questions about the causes.
But, Stephen is fiercely loyal.
Divulges nothing.
He accidentally fell, bumped in to something,
burnt himself.
But, we know the truth.

When I leave Stephen
a mother, myself, to be,
he brings me a ring, in a box, with a yellow stone
to say thank you.

Questions!!
How did this destitute child come by this?
I accept and make no challenge.

Stephen continues to sit on the icy steps, with his sisters.
So very sad.
There are hundreds of thousands of Stephens out there.

Out Of the Mouths of Babes

My little, Australian granddaughter, Caya, aged 15 months, has just spent three weeks with us and has now gone to Gothenburg to spend time with her Swedish grandparents. It's been wonderful, quality time filled with joyous activities: Sandsend, Robin Hoods Bay, Goathland, Whitby and Thornton le Dale.

We miss her and my son and daughter in law but look forward to Xmas with them in Sydney.

I have an adopted little granddaughter, called Evie, who lives in Newcastle, aged nearly seven but with the wisdom of an adult. This is what she said to me when she discovered Caya had left.

"Don't be sad June, life goes on. One of my friends, Olivia, moved away and I miss her. It's been a long time and I'll never see her again. She lives in Manchester and I live in England, well Newcastle mainly. You can still have fun. Make up some games and distract yourself. See if that works. Love you and miss you. You'll be okay, I promise you. Life's not going to end anyways."

What can I say? Feeling better already just listening to

Evie.

Remember she is seven in August.

"Maddie's Big Day" and "A Mother's Love."

"Come on bonnie lass," said Mrs. Jenkins, "it's time for bed, you have a long day ahead tomorrow, so get washed and brush your teeth."

"Ok Mam," replied Maddie as she dashed upstairs.

That night she tossed and turned, unable to sleep, due to the excitement she felt about the big day awaiting her.

She was in a very deep slumber, however, when she heard her mother's voice, "Wake up sleepy head, it's time to get ready."

Maddie leapt out of bed and dashed to the bathroom for a shower and then got dressed into her clean, ironed uniform.

She was in the Air Training Corps, Seaham Squadron, and today they were bound for the Royal Airforce, Topcliffe, to fly in a glider. Maddie had never flown in an aircraft before, and she could hardly contain her excitement.

"Now don't gobble your breakfast," Mum urged, "they won't leave without you."

The minibus stopped outside her house and she kissed Mum before dashing to meet her friends.

Throughout the journey, to the airfield, the cadets talked ten to the dozen about the pending day's flying. The atmosphere on the bus was truly electric. Such excitement.

On arrival at RAF Topcliffe, they were met by a member of the flying team, who welcomed them and informed them of the flying programme for the day.

There were a number of mandatory tests to complete before the cadets would be allowed to fly. These consisted of a weight check, examination of cadet medical records, how to egress the aircraft, in the unlikely event of an emergency and watching a flight safety film. Once completed they would be bussed out to the flight line. All the participants were kitted out in a flight suit, and they imagined themselves as Top Gun pilots. The uncontrolled chatter was incessant.

As the cadets were about to board the flight line transport, an officer on the squadron approached the adult accompanying them, informing him that Maddie's medical declaration indicated she was asthmatic. The officer asked her if she had brought her inhaler, as this had to be on hand, if required. She told him that she had not used one for about 6 months and so had left it at home. Unfortunately, the officer then informed her that she could not fly without the inhaler in case she had an attack whilst airborne.

Maddie was devastated and burst into tears. She could not believe that, after all the anticipation, she was not going to be able to fly. Her dream was shattered.

The thoughtful officer asked if an inhaler could be bought over the counter, at a pharmacy, in nearby Thirsk. A short telephone call to the chemist resulted in a negative response as Maddie's inhaler could only be obtained by prescription. All seemed lost and she was convinced that was the end of her dream.

It was suggested to Maddie that she might telephone home and speak to her mother to see if anyone could bring the inhaler to the airfield.

"I can't ask me mam," Maddie replied tearfully, "she has to look after my younger brother as my dad died a couple of years ago of cancer."

The officer decided that a phone call to Maddie's mother was still worth a try.

An hour later a response from the Guard Room, at the entrance to the base, informed him that an inhaler had been delivered, by a lady who had a just driven post haste, from Seaham. A two hour round trip!

All Maddie's friends cheered when she was finally authorised to fly.

When the time came for her to take to the air, she was shaking with excitement. A member of the squadron staff strapped her into the cockpit and within seconds she was off and soaring up into the blue sky. Maddie looked in wonderment at the earth below, it was more beautiful than she could ever have imagined. Everywhere she looked she could see clouds, the Cleveland Hills, tiny cars rushing along the A19 and The Pennines in the distance. Maddie wished it could last forever. The air was so smooth, and she felt as though she could touch the clouds which had begun to gather. Suddenly, and most unexpectedly, a ray of sunlight flashed into the cockpit coming to rest on its occupant. A true sign from above?

As the aircraft began to descend, the pilot explained they were going to land shortly, and he pointed out where the airfield was. They lined up on the approach and, before they knew it, they were back on the ground.

The smile on Maddie's face was magic. She had finally fulfilled her dream of flying.

All the cadets lined up as the officer presented them with their Wings to wear on their uniforms. No one was prouder than Maddie.

Before they left for home, the officer spoke to Maddie

and suggested she give her mum a big hug when she got home.

"Yes, I will sir," she gratefully replied.

That evening Maddie couldn't wait to share with her mum the excitement of the big day, and, later, tucked up in bed, Maddie said, "Thanks Mam, I love you lots." Mrs. Jenkins kissed her daughter goodnight as she closed the bedroom door.

As Maddie began to drift off to sleep, she whispered, "Well dad, I did it, and I know you were up there somewhere ... watching me."

This is a true story which happened very recently at Topcliffe where my husband flies.

Flowers On the Farm

We sit in the big barn, overlooking the stunning Esk Valley. What a view, what a perfect place to just be.

The farm belongs to Audrey, our teacher, and, in all weathers, we sit there being creative. Sometimes the barn shutters rattle and clatter vigorously, particularly on a windy day, the farm being quite elevated and exposed, and Audrey's washing clings desperately to the line, extra pegs required and very necessary.

In the summer the barn sides are open, and a gentle breeze flows around, warming and inspiring us.

This group of ladies meets quite regularly, throughout the year, to arrange flowers.

The Christmas season is particularly wonderful, and, after a full day's workshop, we noisily depart, car boots piled high with our creations for all to see and appreciate, shared ideas and suggestions. Christmas wreaths for doors and churchyards; table decorations displaying baubles and candles; star shapes of silver and bronze; liberal use of free hedgerow foliage in an abundance of colours and natural hues.

A truly satisfying hobby shared with like - minded people

encouraging a tangible feeling of togetherness and comradeship through shared experience.

What better way to bring a smile to someone's face than by giving flowers, and, a personal arrangement, specifically for them, meaning so much more.

Flowers hold such significance throughout our lives and, if you consider the major events when they are bestowed, they are definitely a great gift, sweetly perfumed and visually appealing.

The celebration of a new life with flowers for the mother; wedding bouquets and often the church is also festooned at the altar, pew ends and entrance archways; funeral farewells where, frequently, the departed's favourites are chosen. The Christmas and Harvest seasons will see our churches garlanded with fruits and flowers and, of course, what could be better than a birthday bouquet? Sadness and sickness can also be alleviated with a thoughtful posy. The list goes on.

FLOWERS a gift from God and what a dull place the world would be without them.

Local Legend

CLAIRE.

Always there.

Best friend.

Good mate.

Listening ear.

Willing helper

And supporter.

CLAIRE

Caring.

Concerned.

Creator of her

Social hub.

CLAIRE

Inspirational.

Dedicated'

Slightly crazy.

Iron Man achiever.

Leader of her pack.

If you know Claire
Count yourself lucky.
One of life's
Little treasures.

CLAIRE
Always there.

Hope

Hope is a promise
On the horizon
And way, way beyond.

Hope emerges from
The depths of despair
Into the sunlight.

Hope is that the Earth
Will survive mankind's
Destructive footprint.

Hope desires and inspires
Always the giver
Makes no demands.

Hope is just knowing
And trusting that love
Always will prevail.

My abiding hope is
For a miracle match
That buys precious time.

The Feeling of Fear

I know what it is now.
I recognise it instantly.
That feeling of fear.

Not of what you would imagine.
Not of spiders,
Or fear of heights.
Nor of drowning.

No, this is quite a different fear.
One that pervades your heart and soul.
Grinding, gripping, twisting, invading.
Never releasing its calculating clutches.
Damaging and destructive.
Ever present. No respite.

It's there when you awake,
It interrupts your daily tasks.
Always, always there at night.
Penetrating the sleep zone.

Disturbing. Antagonistic.
Writhing and relentless.

This real fear
Fears the present
And certainly the uncertain future.
Five years on.
The prediction.
The death sentence.
Two to go.

Unanswered questions.
What about the future?
How much time do we have?
What about my son, the sufferer?
And his precious family?
Who will foot the bill
For the drugs that are his lifeline?

No answers yet.
Just hope.
And faith.

Wilf

Sadly, many people have lost loved ones recently, too many, but my loss is not attributed to Coronavirus.

For 34 years I have lived next to Wilf and Joy, dear neighbours. Although Wilf was 90 years old, and had a frail body, his Spirit, and outlook on life, were those of a 21-year-old. He was a dear man who meant a lot to me.

We had incredible fun over the years, socialising and visiting new venues for coffee and meals. We could always rely on Joy and Wilf to suggest interesting, and amazing, places to dine, and, you could be quite sure Wilf would have to select his Sticky Toffee Pudding for dessert. (He had quite a sweet tooth.)

Wilf had an amazing talent as a professional artist but was also proficient in window dressing, sign writing and pyrography (wood burning) and he frequented craft fairs where he would sell his handiwork. My home has many of his master pieces and, each Christmas, we have been privileged to receive hand designed cards which I treasure. He painted a most beautiful portrait of my 2 Grandsons. Such talent!

The day of his funeral was glorious, and the sun shone.

We stood outside the Catholic Church, at Egton Bridge, where he attended Primary School. His father, Urban Harrison, had helped to build the church, so it was particularly appropriate that Wilf should take his last journey there.

The wonderful view over the Esk Valley, from the rear of my house, means that I overlook Wilf and Joy's bungalow. I see his little greenhouse and raised vegetable beds where he grew his potatoes, onions, lettuce and tomatoes. The last of the leeks recently being lifted and only the parsley clump remaining. If I look carefully, I think I can see Wilf digging away, proudly nurturing his crop, and, know for sure, he will be there in Spirit, overseeing his kitchen garden and keeping Joy company.

A life well lived and extensively travelled, 66 years happily married, 6 children, 9 grandchildren and 11 great grandchildren. He has left behind a legacy of love and cherished memories and I, for one, will miss him.

Wilf Harrison, our treasured neighbour, in Sleights, who sadly passed away.

Printed in Great Britain
by Amazon

29203392R00096